Florida
NOTARY PRIMER

The NNA's Handbook for Florida Notaries

Twenty-first Edition

Published by:

National Notary Association
9350 De Soto Avenue
Chatsworth, CA 91311-4926
Telephone: (800) 876-6827
Fax: (818) 700-0920
Website: NationalNotary.org
Email: nna@NationalNotary.org

©2023 National Notary Association
ALL RIGHTS RESERVED. No part of this book may be reproduced in any form without permission in writing from the publisher.

The information in this *Primer* is correct and current at the time of its publication, although new laws, regulations and rulings may subsequently affect the validity of certain sections. This information is provided to aid comprehension of state Notary Public requirements and should not be construed as legal advice. Please consult an attorney for inquiries relating to legal matters.

Twenty-first Edition ©2023
First Edition ©1982

ISBN: 978-1-59767-317-4

Table of Contents

Introduction 1

The Notary Appointment 2

Screening the Signer 8

Reviewing the Document 20

Notary Acts 26

Recordkeeping 45

Notary Certificate and Seal 48

In-Person Electronic Notarization and Remote Online
Notarization 53

Misconduct, Fines and Penalties 62

Florida Laws Pertaining to Notaries Public 67

About the NNA 109

Index 110

Have a Tough Notary Question?

If you were a National Notary Association member, you could get the answer to that difficult question. Join the NNA® and your membership includes access to the NNA® Hotline* and live Notary experts providing the latest Notary information regarding laws, rules and regulations.

Hours
Monday – Friday   5:00 a.m.–6:30 p.m. (PT)
Saturday   5:00 a.m.–5:00 p.m. (PT)

NNA® Hotline Toll-Free Phone Number: 1-888-876-0827

After hours you can leave a message or email our experts at Hotline@NationalNotary.org and they will respond the next business day.

*Access to the NNA® Hotline is for National Notary Association members and NNA® Hotline subscribers only. Call and become a member today.

Introduction

You are to be commended on your interest in Florida Notary law! Purchasing the *Florida Notary Primer* identifies you as a conscientious professional who takes your official duties seriously.

In few fields is the expression "more to it than meets the eye" truer than in Notary law. What often appears on the surface to be a simple procedure may, in fact, have important legal considerations.

The purpose of the *Florida Notary Primer* is to provide you with a resource to help decipher the many intricate laws that affect notarization. In so doing, the *Primer* will acquaint you with all of the important aspects of Florida's Notary laws and with prudent Notary practices in general.

The *Florida Notary Primer* begins with informative chapters on how to obtain your commission, what tools the Notary needs, and critical steps in notarization. We also take you through the myriad of Notary laws and put them in easy-to-understand terms. Every section of the law is analyzed and explained, as well as topics not covered by Florida law but nonetheless of vital concern to you as a Notary.

Whether you're about to be commissioned for the first time or a longtime Notary, we're sure that the *Florida Notary Primer* will provide you with new insight and understanding.

Milton G. Valera
Chairman
National Notary Association

The Notary Appointment

THE NOTARY COMMISSION

Application for Commission

Qualifications. To become a Notary in Florida, the applicant must be a legal Florida resident at least 18 years old (FS 117.01[1]).

Mandatory Course. Within one year of applying, each first time applicant must take and pass an interactive or classroom course on Notary duties of at least three hours from a private or public agency approved by the Governor's office. A certificate of course completion must be included with the application. Applicants renewing their commissions are not required to take another course (FS 668.50[11] [b]]).

Application. Each applicant must complete the official application provided by the Department of State. The application contains both the Notary's oath of office and the affidavit of good character (FS 117.01[2]).

Affidavit of Good Character. An affidavit attesting to the applicant's good character must be completed by someone unrelated to him or her who has known the applicant for at least one year. This affidavit is included on the Notary application form (FS 117.01[2]).

Application Fee. The total fee for a Notary commission applicant is $39 — $10 of which is the commission fee, $25 is the application fee and $4 a surcharge to be used by the Governor to educate and assist Notaries (FS 117.01[2]).

Permanent Residents. A permanent resident who applies for a Notary commission must also file with his or her application a recorded Declaration of Domicile (FS 117.01[1]).

Fictitious Names. An applicant may not submit a fictitious or assumed name except for a regularly used nickname on the application for commission (FS 117.01[2]).

Previous Convictions. If the Notary has indicated on the application that he or she has been convicted of a felony, a written statement describing the felony, along with a Certificate of Restoration of Civil Rights, must be submitted (FS 117.01[2]).

Application Misstatement. The Governor may suspend a Notary's commission for material false statements on the Notary Public application (FS 117.01[4]).

Notary Bond

Requirement. Every Florida Notary is required to obtain a bond of $7,500 payable to any person financially damaged as a result of the Notary's misconduct (FS 117.01[7][a]).

Online Notary. If a Notary registers to become an online Notary, a $25,000 bond is required, and this bond satisfies the requirement of the $7,500 bond (FS 117.225[6]).

Filing the Bond. The bond must be filed with the Department of State with the commission application, the oath of office and affidavit of good character (FS 117.01[2]).

Surety. The surety for the Notary's bond must be a state-licensed bonding company. Notaries may not offer their own assets, or the assets of a friend, relative or employer, as a surety (FS 117.01[7][a]).

Claims. Whenever a claim is made against the Notary and any funds are paid out on his or her behalf, the bonding company must notify the Governor of the circumstances leading to the claim (FS 117.01[8]).

Protects Public. The Notary bond protects the public from a Notary's misconduct. The bond does not protect the Notary. The bond's surety is normally a bonding company that agrees to pay damages to anyone who suffers financially because of the Notary's improper acts, intentional or not, in the event that the Notary does not have the financial resources to pay these damages. The surety will seek compensation from the Notary for any damages it has to pay out on the Notary's behalf.

Liable for All Damages. A Notary and the surety company bonding the Notary may be sued by any person who has been damaged by the Notary's errors. The surety is liable only up to the amount of the bond ($7,500 in Florida), but a Notary may be found liable for any amount of money.

Oath of Office

Requirement. Every Florida Notary is required to take an official oath that he or she will honestly and faithfully carry out the duties of office. As part of the oath, the Notary must swear that he or she has read the laws regarding Notaries Public (FS 117.01–117.20) and knows the duties and responsibilities of being a Notary (FS 117.01[3] and [7][a]).

Filing the Oath. The oath is a written statement included on the application for commission. Since the statement is signed under penalties of perjury, signing the statement has the same effect as taking an oral oath (FS 117.01[2]).

Jurisdiction

Statewide. Notaries may perform official acts throughout the state of Florida but not beyond the state borders. A Notary may not witness a signing outside of Florida and then return to the state to perform the notarization. All parts of a notarial act must be performed at the same time and place within the state of Florida (FS 117.01[1]).

Term of Office

Four-Year Term. A Notary's term of office is four years, beginning with the date specified on the commission certificate and ending at midnight on the expiration date (FS 117.01[1]).

Reappointment

Procedure. No person will automatically be reappointed at the end of the four-year term. A Notary who wishes to renew his or her commission must complete the same application process as a new Notary (FS 117.01[6]).

Law Enforcement Officers

May Act as Notaries. Law enforcement and correctional officers, including probation officers, traffic accident investigators and traffic infraction enforcement officers, have the authority to act as Notaries Public whenever they are engaged in official duties. That is, they may take acknowledgments and administer oaths and affirmations; however, they may not perform marriages (FS 117.10).

Civil-Law Notaries

Qualifications. To qualify as a civil-law Notary, a person must be a member in good standing of the Florida Bar, have practiced law for at least five years and been appointed a civil-law Notary by the Department of State (FS 118.10).

For more information on becoming a civil-law Notary, contact the Department of State at (850) 245-6975 or the Florida Bar.

Authority. A civil-law Notary has all of the authority of a state-commissioned Notary Public but may also perform "authentic acts" which confirm the text of an instrument, the signatures of the transacting parties and the signature and seal of the civil-law Notary (FS 118.10).

The civil-law Notary may transact business and execute notarial acts for use in a jurisdiction outside of the United States unless the U.S. Department of State has determined that the particular jurisdiction does not have diplomatic relations with the United

States or if trade with the specific jurisdiction is prohibited under the Trading with the Enemy Act of 1917 (50 U.S. Code, Sec. 1, et. seq.) (FS 118.10).

'Protocol' Required. Similar to the Notary's official journal of acts, a "protocol" is a register of all transactions performed by the civil-law Notary. A civil-law Notary's official acts are to be recorded in the protocol (FS 118.10).

Regulations. The Department of State may adopt regulations governing civil-law Notaries. However, the Department of State may not regulate, discipline or establish educational requirements for civil law Notaries unless in agreement with the Florida Bar (FS 118.10).

Change of Address

Notification. Whenever a Notary changes the address or telephone number of his or her principal place of business or home, the Notary must inform the Department of State of the change. To act as a Florida Notary, the Notary must maintain state residency throughout the entire term of the appointment (FS 117.01[2]).

The Governor may suspend a Notary Public for failure to report a change of business or residence address or telephone number. The information must be submitted in writing within 60 days to the Department of State (FS 117.01[4][g]).

Moving Out of State. A Notary Public who moves out of state must resign the commission (FS 117.01[5][b]). (See "Resignation," page 7.)

Change of Name

Notification Required. A Notary who changes his or her name must file a name change form with the Secretary of State within 60 days of the change. The form shall include the new name and a specimen of the new signature. A rider to the Notary's bond, the old commission paper and a $25 fee must accompany the application. The Notary may continue to notarize in the old name until receipt of an amended commission — showing the new name — from the Department of State or the passage of 60 days, whichever comes first (FS 117.05[9]).

The Governor may suspend a Notary Public commission for failure to submit the required information to request an amended commission due to a name change (FS 117.01[4][g]).

Resignation

Required. Resignation is required when the Governor requires it, when a Notary fails to maintain residency in the state or when the Notary no longer wishes to act as a Notary (FS 117.01[5][b]).

Procedure. If a Notary Public wishes to resign the commission, he or she must send a signed letter of resignation to the Governor and include his or her original Notary commission certificate. The Notary should also include their mailing address because the Governor will send them an acceptance letter acknowledging their resignation. Unless otherwise requested, the Notary Public must also destroy his or her seal and/or embosser (FS 117.01[5][b]).

Change of Criminal Record

Notification Required. Any conviction or other change in a Notary's criminal record must be reported to the Secretary of State within 60 days (FS 117.01[2]).

Lost or Misplaced Commission Certificate

A duplicate commission certificate of one that is lost or misplaced may be requested from the Department of State, Bureau of Notaries Public (RMN).

Screening the Signer

SCREENING BASICS

Personal Appearance

Requirement. The person requesting notarization must personally appear before the Notary at the time of the notarization. This means that the Notary and signer must be face to face when the notarization takes place. For approved remote online notarizations, the Notary and signer meet via real-time audio-video technology. Notarizations may never be performed over the telephone (FS 117.107[9]).

Direct Communication

Requirement. The Notary must be able to communicate directly with the individual for whom a Notary act is being performed in a language they both understand. Therefore, a Notary cannot use an interpreter to communicate with a signer because of a lack of direct communication. If a Notary can't establish direct communication, the signer should be directed to a Notary who speaks their language.

Willingness

Confirmation. The Notary should make every effort to confirm that the signer is acting willingly. To confirm willingness, the Notary need only ask document signers if they are signing of their own free will. If a signer does or says anything that makes the Notary think the signer is being pressured to sign, the Notary should refuse to notarize.

Awareness

Confirmation. Florida law prohibits a Notary from notarizing a signature on a document if it appears that the person is mentally incapable of understanding the nature and effect of the document at the time of notarization (FS 117.107[5]).

The Notary should make every effort to confirm that the signer is aware of what is taking place. To confirm awareness, the Notary simply makes a layperson's judgment about the signer's ability to understand what is happening. A document signer who cannot respond intelligibly in a simple conversation with the Notary should not be considered sufficiently aware to sign at that moment. If the notarization is taking place in a medical environment, the signer's doctor can be consulted for a professional opinion. Otherwise, if the signer's awareness is in doubt, the Notary must refuse to notarize.

Mental Incapacitation. Florida law specifically prohibits a Notary from taking the acknowledgment or administering an oath to a person whom the Notary knows to have been adjudicated mentally incapacitated by a court of competent jurisdiction, where the acknowledgment or oath necessitates the exercise of a right that has been removed and where the person has not been restored to capacity (FS 117.107[4]).

Identifying Document Signers

Procedure. In notarizing any signature, whether by acknowledgment or jurat, Florida law requires the Notary to positively identify the document signer. The following three methods of identification are acceptable (FS 117.05[5]):

1. The Notary's *personal knowledge* of the signer's identity (see "Personal Knowledge of Identity," page 10);

2. Reliable *identification documents* or ID cards (see "Identification Documents [ID Cards]," pages 11–12); or

3. The oath or affirmation of one personally known *credible identifying witness* or two *credible identifying witnesses* identified by identification documents (see "Credible Identifying Witness[es]," pages 12–15).

Indicate on Notary Certificate. The Notary must indicate on the certificate of acknowledgment or jurat the method of identification of the signer — that is, whether the Notary relied upon personal knowledge or satisfactory evidence and the type of evidence produced (FS 117.05[5]).

Personal Knowledge of Identity

Definition. The safest and most reliable method of identifying a document signer is for the Notary to depend upon his or her own personal knowledge of the signer's identity. Personal knowledge means familiarity with an individual resulting from interactions with that person over a period of time sufficient to eliminate every reasonable doubt that the person has the identity claimed. The familiarity should come from association with the individual in relation to other people and should be based upon a chain of circumstances surrounding the individual (FS 117.05[5][a]).

Florida law does not specify how long a Notary must be acquainted with an individual before personal knowledge of identity may be claimed. The Notary's common sense must prevail. In general, the longer the Notary is acquainted with a person, and the more interactions that the Notary has had with that person, the more likely the individual is personally known.

For instance, the Notary might safely regard a friend since childhood as personally known, but would be foolish to consider a person met for the first time the previous day as such. Whenever the Notary has a reasonable doubt about a signer's identity, that individual should not be considered personally known and the identification should be made through either a credible identifying witness or reliable identification documents.

Identification Documents (ID Cards)

Acceptable Identification Documents. A Notary may identify a document signer through any one of the identification documents listed below. The document must 1) be current or if expired, issued within the past five years, and 2) bear a serial or other identifying number (FS 117.05[5][b][2]):

- Florida driver's license or identification card issued by the Department of Highway Safety and Motor Vehicles.

- U.S. passport issued by the U.S. Department of State.

- Foreign passport if stamped by the U.S. Citizenship and Immigration Services (USCIS).

- Driver's license or non-driver's ID issued by another U.S. state or territory.

- Driver's license officially issued in Mexico or Canada.

- U.S. military ID.

- Inmate ID issued on or after January 1, 1991, by the Florida Department of Corrections or Federal Bureau of Prisons (but only to identify prisoners in custody).

- A sworn, written statement from a sworn law enforcement officer explaining that an inmate's IDs were confiscated upon incarceration, and that the person named in the document is the person whose signature is to be notarized.

- Permanent resident card, or "green card," issued by the U.S. Citizenship and Immigration Services (USCIS).

- A veteran health identification card issued by U.S. Dept. of Veterans Affairs.

Unacceptable Identification Documents. Unacceptable ID cards for identifying acknowledgers include, but are not limited to: birth certificates, Social Security cards, credit cards and driver's licenses without photographs.

Multiple Identification. While one good identification document or card may be sufficient to identify a signer, the Notary may ask for more.

Credible Identifying Witness(es)

Purpose. When a document signer is not personally known to the Notary and is not able to present reliable identification documents, that signer may be identified through the oath (or affirmation) of one or two credible identifying witnesses (FS 117.05[5][b]).

Qualifications and Identification. Every credible identifying witness must personally know the document signer. If there is only one credible identifying witness to identify the signer, that witness must also be personally known by the Notary. This establishes a chain of personal knowledge from the signer to the credible identifying witness to the Notary.

If there are two credible identifying witnesses available to identify the signer, these witnesses need not be personally known to the Notary but must be identified through an acceptable identification document listed under "Identification Documents (ID Cards)," see pages 11–12 (FS 117.05[5][b]).

Oath (Affirmation) for Credible Identifying Witness. To ensure truthfulness, the Notary must obtain a sworn, written statement from each credible identifying witness that the person signing the document is the person named in the document and that the signer is personally known to the witness (FS 117.05[5][b][1]).

The sworn written statement of one credible witness personally known to the Notary or the swoon written statement of two credible witnesses whose identities are proven to the Notary upon the presentation of satisfactory evidence that each of the following is true (FS 117.05[5][b][1]):

1. The person whose signature is to be notarized is the person named in the document.

2. The person whose signature is to be notarized is personally known to the witness.

3. That it is the reasonable belief of the witness that it would be very difficult or impossible for the person whose signature is to be notarized to obtain another form of identification.

4. The person whose signature is to be notarized does not possess any of the acceptable identification documents.

5. The witness does not have a financial interest in the document and is not named in the document.

Written Statement. If there is space on the document, the credible identifying witness's statement may be typed on the notarized document itself. If the statement is on a separate sheet of paper, the Notary should keep it for his or her records. The following wording is suggested for one credible identifying witness:

Under penalty of perjury, I declare that the person appearing before _____ (name of Notary) is personally known to me as _____ (name of person whose signature is to be notarized) and is the person named in the document requiring notarization.

_____ (Date)
_____ (Signature of witness)

State of Florida

County of _____

Sworn to (or affirmed) and subscribed before me by means of [ ] physical presence or [ ] online notarization, this _____ (numeric date) day of _____ (month), _____ (year), by _____ (name of person making statement).

_____ (Signature of Notary)   (Seal of Notary)
_____ (Name of Notary, printed, typed or stamped)

Personally Known ____ or Produced Identification ____

Type of Identification Produced _____

The following wording is recommended for two credible identifying witnesses:

Under the penalties of perjury, I declare that the person appearing before_____ (name of Notary) is personally known to me as _____ (name of person whose signature is to be notarized) and is the person named in the document requiring notarization; that I believe that this person does not possess the required identification; that I believe it would be difficult or impossible for this person to obtain such identification; and that I do not have a financial interest in and am not a party to the underlying transaction.

_____ (Date)

_____ (Signature of first witness)

_____ (Date)

_____ (Signature of second witness)

State of Florida

County of _____

Sworn to (or affirmed) and subscribed before me by means of [ ] physical presence or [ ]online notarization, this _____ (numeric date) day of _____ (month), _____ (year), by _____ and _____ (names of credible witnesses making statements).

_____ (Signature of Notary)   (Seal of Notary)

_____ (Name of Notary, printed, typed or stamped)

Personally Known ____ or Produced Identification ____

Type of Identification Produced _____

Personally Known ____ or Produced Identification ____

Type of Identification Produced _____

Signature in Notary's Journal. The prudent Notary will record the name, address and signature of each credible identifying witness in a journal. The Notary should also indicate how the witness was identified, either by the Notary's personal knowledge (required for one credible identifying witness) or through acceptable identification documents (required for two credible identifying witnesses).

Indicate on Certificate. The Notary must indicate on the certificate the method used to identify the signer (FS 117.05[5]). To indicate reliance upon a credible identifying witness or witnesses, the Notary should select the phrase "Produced Identification," and after "Type of Identification Produced" write in "credible identifying witness(es)".

Notarization. A Notary may then notarize this signature but should take extra care to avoid any problems. As with any notarization, the Notary must determine the signer's willingness to sign and whether or not the signer understands the purpose of the document.

Notarizing for One Who Directs the Notary to Sign

Persons with a Disability. If a person cannot sign a document due to a physical disability, he or she may direct the Notary to sign on his or her behalf (FS 117.05[14][d]).

Procedure. The person with the disability must be in the presence of the Notary when directing the Notary to sign a document on his or her behalf. The Notary must then sign the document in the presence of two impartial witnesses.

After signing the name of the person, the Notary must write below the signature the following statement: "Signature affixed by Notary pursuant to Section 117.05(14), Florida Statutes," and also state in the Notary certificate the circumstances of the signing (FS 117.05[14][d]).

> Sworn to (or affirmed) before me by means of [ ] physical presence or [ ] online notarization, this _____ day of _____ (month), _____ (year), by _____ (name of person making statement), and subscribed by _____ (name of Notary) at the direction of and in the presence of (name of person making statement), and in the presence of these witnesses: _____ (Names of witnesses).
>
> _____ (Signature of Notary)   (Seal of Notary)

Identification of Principal. The Notary must positively identify the principal — the person directing the Notary to sign — through personal knowledge, credible identifying witness(es) or ID cards.

Certificates. The following certificates are set out by Florida law for performing a notarization for a person with a disability who directs the Notary to sign on his or her behalf (FS 117.05[14] [e]):

- For an Acknowledgment in an Individual Capacity:

    State of Florida

    County of _____

    The foregoing instrument was acknowledged before me by means of [ ] physical presence or [ ] online notarization, this _____ day of _____ (month), _____ (year), by _____ (name of person acknowledging), and subscribed by _____ (name of Notary) at the direction of and in the presence of (name of person acknowledging), and in the presence of these witnesses: _____ (Names of witnesses).

    _____ (Signature of Notary)   (Seal of Notary)

    _____ (Name of Notary, printed, typed or stamped)

    Personally known _____ OR produced identification _____

    Type of identification produced _____

- For a jurat:

    State of Florida

    County of _____

    Sworn to (or affirmed) and subscribed before me this _____ (numeric date) day of _____ (month), _____ (year), by _____ (name of person making statement) and subscribed by _____ (name of Notary) at the direction of and in the presence of (name of person making statement), and in the presence of these witnesses:

    _____ (printed name of witness)

    _____ (printed name of witness)

_____ (Signature of Notary Public - State of Florida)

_____ (Print, Type or Stamp Commissioned Name of Notary Public)

Journal Entry. The prudent Notary will record the specific circumstances of the notarization in a journal and ask all persons involved to sign the journal as well.

Notarizing for the Blind

Read Document. A Notary may not notarize for a blind person without first reading the document to the person. The reading should be verbatim. However, to avoid the unauthorized practice of law, the Notary must not attempt to explain the document (FS 117.05[14][a]).

Signature by Mark

Mark Serves as Signature. A person who cannot sign his or her name because of illiteracy or disability may instead use a mark — an "X" for example — as a signature, as long as there are two witnesses to the making of the mark (FS 117.05[14] [b].

Witnesses. In order for a mark to be acknowledged or sworn to before a Notary, two witnesses should sign the document (e.g. "John Q. Smith, Witness") and the Notary's journal. The Notary should print legibly the marker's name beside the mark on the document in the following manner (FS 117.05[14] [b]):

John   X   Doe

His Mark

Signature by Mark Certificate. A mark is generally considered a signature under law, as long as it is properly witnessed. Florida law provides special Notary certificates for persons signing by mark (FS 117.05[14][c]):

- For an Acknowledgment in an Individual Capacity:

    _____ First Name _____ Last Name

    _____ His or Her Mark

State of Florida

County of _____

The foregoing instrument was acknowledged before me by means of [ ] physical presence or [ ] online notarization, this _____ day of _____ (month), _____ (year), by _____ (name of person), who signed with a mark in the presence of these witnesses: _____ (Names of witnesses).

_____ (Signature of Notary)   (Seal of Notary)

_____ (Name of Notary, printed, typed or stamped)

Personally known _____ OR produced identification _____

Type of identification produced _____

- The following notarial certificate is sufficient for the purpose of an oath or affirmation when a person signs with a mark:

State of Florida

County of _____

Sworn to (or affirmed) and subscribed before me this _____ (numeric date) day of _____ (month), _____ (year), by _____ (name of person making statement), who signed with a mark in the presence of these witnesses: _____ (printed name of witness one)

_____ (printed name of witness two)

_____ (Signature of Notary Public - State of Florida)

_____ (Print, Type or Stamp Commissioned Name of Notary Public)

Personally Known ____ OR Produced Identification ____

Type of Identification Produced: _____

Notarizing for Minors

Under Age 18. Generally, persons must reach the age of majority before they can handle their own legal affairs and sign documents for themselves. In Florida, the age of majority is 18. Normally, parents or guardians will sign on a minor's behalf. In certain cases, where minors are engaged in business transactions or serving as court witnesses, they may lawfully sign documents and have their signatures notarized.

Include Age Next to Signature. When notarizing for a minor, the Notary should ask the young signer to write his or her age next to the signature to alert any person relying upon the document that the signer is a minor. The Notary is not required to verify the minor signer's age.

Identification. The method for identifying a minor is the same as that for an adult. However, because minors often do not possess acceptable identification documents, such as driver's licenses or passports, determining the identity of a minor can be a problem. In Florida, anyone 12 years of age or older may be issued a state non-driver's ID, which the Notary may use as identification.

If the minor does not have an acceptable ID, then the other methods of identifying signers must be used, either the Notary's personal knowledge of the minor or the oath of a credible identifying witness or witnesses who can identify the minor. (See "Credible Identifying Witness[es]," pages 12–15.)

Screening the Signer | 19

Reviewing the Document

DOCUMENT CONTENT

Incomplete Documents

Do Not Notarize. Florida Notaries are specifically prohibited from notarizing a signature on a document that is incomplete (FS 117.107[10]).

Any blanks in a document should be filled in by the signer. If the blanks are inapplicable and intended to be left unfilled, the signer should determine whether to line through the blank or to write "Not Applicable" or "N/A". The Notary should never provide advice on how to complete the document. This would be considered the unauthorized practice of law.

An endorsement or assignment in blank of a negotiable or nonnegotiable note and the assignment in blank of any instrument given as security for such note is not considered incomplete.

Notaries are also specifically prohibited from signing and sealing blank Notary certificates and trusting another person to fill them out (FS 117.107[3]).

Disqualifying Interest

Impartiality. Notaries are appointed by the state to be impartial, disinterested witnesses whose screening duties help ensure the integrity of important legal and commercial transactions. Lack of impartiality by a Notary throws doubt on the integrity and lawfulness of any transaction. A Notary must never notarize his or her own signature, or notarize in a transaction in which the Notary has a financial or beneficial interest (FS 117.107[12]).

Financial or Beneficial Interest. A Notary should not perform any notarization related to a transaction in which that Notary has a direct financial or beneficial interest (FS 117.107[12]).

A financial or beneficial interest exists when the Notary is individually named as a principal or beneficiary in a financial transaction or when the Notary receives an advantage, right, privilege, property or fee valued in excess of the lawfully prescribed Notary fee.

Exceptions. A Notary who notarizes for an employer that receives a benefit from a transaction is not considered to have a disqualifying interest unless he or she receives a benefit other than his or her salary and the statutory fee for notarization. In addition, a Notary who is an attorney does not have a disqualifying interest in notarizing the signature of a client unless he or she is a party to or named in the document (FS 117.107[12]).

Any challenged case of disqualifying financial or beneficial interest would be decided in court on its own merits. Thus, it is always safest for a Notary to have no financial or beneficial interest whatsoever in a transaction regardless of what the law allows.

Relatives. A Notary may not notarize for a spouse, son, daughter, mother or father (FS 117.107[11]).

Refusal of Services

Legal Request for Services. Ideally, as officers appointed to serve the general public, Notaries should honor all lawful and reasonable requests to notarize, regardless of the signer's client or non-client status and without discrimination or personal bias.

However, the Governor's Notary Section has opined that it is not unlawful discrimination for an Employee-Notary to limit service to the customers of a Notary's employer or to transactions that are solely related to the business purposes of the Notary's employer during the Notary's normal working hours (web, FAQ's).

Wills

Do Not Offer Advice. Often, people attempt to draw up wills without benefit of legal counsel and then bring these homemade testaments to a Notary to have them "legalized," expecting the Notary to know how to proceed. In advising or assisting such persons, the Notary risks prosecution for the unauthorized practice of law; the Notary's ill-informed advice may do considerable damage to the affairs of the signer.

Living Wills. Documents that are popularly called "living wills" may be notarized. These are not actually wills at all, but written statements of the signer's wishes concerning medical treatment in the event that the person has an illness or injury and is unable to issue instructions on his or her own behalf.

Unauthorized Practice of Law

Do Not Assist Others with Legal Matters. A nonattorney Notary may not give legal advice or accept fees for legal advice. The nonattorney Notary may not assist a signer in drafting, preparing, selecting, completing or understanding a document or transaction. The Notary should not fill in blank spaces in the text of a document for other persons, tell others what documents they need or how to draft them, or advise others about the legal sufficiency of a document — and especially not for a fee. A Notary may fill in the blanks on the portion of any document containing the Notary certificate. And a Notary, as a private individual, may prepare legal documents that he or she is personally a party to, but the Notary may not then notarize his or her signature on these same documents. Notaries who overstep their authority by advising others on legal matters have committed a felony of the third degree (FS 454.23).

Exceptions. Nonattorney Notaries certified or licensed in a particular field (e.g., real estate, insurance or escrow) may offer advice in that field. Paralegals under the supervision of an attorney may advise others about documents in routine legal matters.

Authentication

Documents Sent Out of State. Documents notarized in Florida and sent to other states may be required to bear proof that the Notary's signature and seal are genuine and that the Notary had authority to act at the time of notarization. This process of proving the genuineness of an official signature and seal is called authentication or legalization.

In Florida, the proof is in the form of an authenticating certificate attached to the notarized document by the Department of State. These certificates are known by different names: certificates of authority, certificates of capacity, certificates of authenticity, certificates of prothonotary and "flags."

An authenticating certificate from the Florida Secretary of State costs $10. It is not the Notary's responsibility to pick up or pay for the certificate of authority. To obtain a certificate of authority, the document signer must submit by mail a written request with the notarized document, a self-addressed, stamped envelope if the document is to be returned by mail, and a check or money order payable to "Department of State" to (FS 117.103):

>   Department of State Division
>   of Corporations *Apostille*
>   Certification
>   P.O. Box 6800
>   Tallahassee, FL 32314-6800
>   (850) 245-6945

Documents Sent Out of Country. If the notarized document is going outside the United States, a chain authentication process may be necessary and additional certificates of authority may have to be obtained from the U.S. Department of State in Washington, D.C., a foreign embassy in Washington, D.C. and a ministry of foreign affairs in the particular foreign nation.

Apostilles and The Hague Convention. Fortunately, over 100 nations, including the United States, subscribe to a treaty that simplifies authentication of notarized documents exchanged between any of the nations. The official name of this treaty, adopted by the Conference on October 5, 1961, is *The Hague Convention Abolishing the Requirement of Legalization for Foreign Public Documents* (for a list of the subscribing countries, visit www.hcch.net/index_en.php).

Under The Hague Convention, only one authenticating certificate, called an *apostille*, is necessary to ensure acceptance of a Notary's signature and stamp in these subscribing countries. (*Apostille* means "notation" in French.)

Apostilles are issued by the Florida Department of State. The procedure and fee are the same as for obtaining an authenticating certificate. To assist the department in determining the correct type of authenticating certificate, any request must include the country of destination.

Foreign Languages

Foreign-Language Documents. Florida Notaries are not expressly prohibited from notarizing non-English documents. As long as the Notary certificate and document signature are in English or in a language the Notary can read, Florida Notaries may notarize foreign-language documents.

However, there are difficulties to consider with foreign-language documents: blatant fraud might go undetected, the U.S. Notary seal might be misinterpreted in another country, and making a journal entry might be difficult.

Foreign-Language Signers. There should always be direct communication between the Notary and document signer, whether in English or another language. The Notary should never rely upon an intermediary or interpreter to determine a signer's willingness or awareness. A third party may have reasons to misrepresent the transaction to the Notary and/or to the signer.

Specifically, Florida law prohibits a Notary from notarizing for a signer who does not speak or understand the English language unless the nature and effect of the document is translated into a language that the signer understands (FS 117.107[6]).

Immigration

Naturalization Certificates. A Notary may only photocopy a certificate of naturalization for lawful purposes. The NNA recommends that a Notary only certify a copy of the certificate if written directions are provided by a U.S. immigration authority.

Advertising

False or Misleading Advertising. A Notary's commission can be suspended if the Notary uses false or misleading advertising to misrepresent the authority, rights and privileges of a Notary. For example, a Notary who represents himself or herself to be an immigration expert and who leads clients to believe that he or she has powers beyond that of a Florida Notary is guilty of false advertising (FS 117.01[4][e]).

Foreign-Language Advertising. A nonattorney Notary advertising Notary services in a foreign language must take steps to guard against misinterpretation of his or her authorized function. Notaries are required to include in any such foreign-language advertisement the following statement in English and in the foreign language (FS 117.05[10]):

I AM NOT AN ATTORNEY LICENSED TO PRACTICE LAW IN THE STATE OF FLORIDA, AND I MAY NOT GIVE LEGAL ADVICE OR ACCEPT FEES FOR LEGAL ADVICE.

The statement must be shown in a conspicuous size and applies to signs and all other forms of written communication (e.g., business cards, printed ads) with the exception of a single desk plaque. If the ad is by radio or television, this statement may be modified but must contain the same information (FS 117.05[10]).

Translation of 'Notary Public.' Literal translation of "Notary Public" into a language other than English (e.g. in Spanish, *Notario Publico* or *Notaria Publica*) is prohibited by law (FS 117.05[11]).

Notary Acts

Authorized Acts

Notaries may perform the following notarizations:

- **Acknowledgments,** certifying that a signer personally appeared before the Notary, was positively identified and acknowledged signing the document (FS 117.04). (See pages 27–32.)

- **Certified Copies.** A Notary may make or supervise the making of a photocopy of a document that is not a vital or public record and attest to the trueness of the copy (FS 117.05[12]). (See pages 32–34.)

- **Inventorying a Safe-Deposit Box,** certifying the contents of a safe-deposit box opened by a financial institution due to non-payment of rental fees (FS 655.94). (See pages 34–35.)

- **Jurats,** certifying that the signer personally appeared before the Notary, was positively identified, signed in the Notary's presence and took an oath or affirmation from the Notary (FS 117.05). (See pages 35–36.)

- **Marriages.** Florida Notaries are authorized to solemnize marriages as long as the couple presents a valid marriage certificate (FS 117.045). (See pages 36–37.)

- **Oaths and Affirmations,** which are solemn promises to a Supreme Being (oath) or solemn promises on one's own personal honor (affirmation) (FS 117.03). (See pages 37–39.)
- **Verifying a Vehicle Identification Number,** or VIN, by physical inspection (FS 319.23). (See pages 41–42.)

Acknowledgments

A Common Notarial Act. Acknowledgments are one of the most common forms of notarization. Typically, they are executed on documents such as deeds and liens affecting the title to real property that will be publicly recorded by a county recorder.

Purpose. In executing an acknowledgment, the Notary certifies three things (FS 117.05[4]–[5]):

1. The signer *personally appeared* before the Notary by physical presence or by means of audio-video communication technology on the date and in the county indicated on the Notary certificate (notarization cannot be based upon a telephone call or a Notary's familiarity with a signature).

2. The signer was *positively identified* by the Notary through either personal knowledge or satisfactory evidence (see "Identifying Document Signers," pages 9–10).

3. The signer *acknowledged* to the Notary that the signature was freely made for the purposes stated in the document. (If a document is willingly signed in the presence of the Notary, this can serve just as well as an oral statement of acknowledgment.)

Certificate for Acknowledgment. For every acknowledgment, the Notary must complete a Notary certificate that includes a statement as to how the signer was identified and that the signer personally appeared before the Notary or appeared remotely through audio-video communication (FS 117.05[4]). (See "Notary Certificate," pages 48–51.)

Florida law provides certificate wording for acknowledgments by persons signing in individual and representative capacities. The authorization of these forms does not prohibit the use of other appropriate wordings (FS 117.05[13] [b][c]).

- Individual Acknowledgment — for an individual signing on his or her own behalf:

    State of Florida

    County of _____

    The foregoing instrument was acknowledged before me by means of ☐ physical presence or ☐ online notarization, this ____ day of _____ (month), ____ (year), by _____ (name of person acknowledging).

    _____ (Signature of Notary)   (Seal of Notary)

    _____ (Name of Notary, printed, typed or stamped)

    Personally known ____ OR produced identification _____

    Type of identification produced _____

- Representative Acknowledgment Certificate — for a corporate officer, trustee, executor, attorney in fact, guardian or other representative acting on behalf of an entity or person:

    State of Florida

    County of _____

    The foregoing instrument was acknowledged before me by means of ☐ physical presence or ☐ online notarization, this ____ day of _____ (month), ____ (year), by _____ (name of person) as (type of authority, e.g. officer, trustee, attorney in fact) for (name of party on behalf of whom instrument was executed).

    _____ (Signature of Notary)   (Seal of Notary)

    _____ (Name of Notary, printed, typed or stamped)

    Personally known ____ OR produced identification ____

    Type of identification produced _____

Short-Form Acknowledgment Certificates. In addition to the preceding certificates, Florida law authorizes the use of several short-form certificates that accommodate signers in various representative capacities. The authorization of these short forms does not prohibit the use of other suitable forms (FS 695.25).

- Individual Acknowledgment Short-Form Certificate — for an individual or individuals signing on his or her behalf:

    State of Florida

    County of _____

    The foregoing instrument was acknowledged before me by means of ☐ physical presence or ☐ online notarization, this _____ (date) by _____ (name of person acknowledging), who is personally known to me or who has produced (type of identification) as identification.

    _____ (Signature of Notary)   (Seal of Notary)

    _____ (Name of Notary, printed, typed or stamped)

- Corporate Acknowledgment Short-Form Certificate — for a corporate officer acting on behalf of a corporation:

    State of Florida

    County of _____

    The foregoing instrument was acknowledged before me by means of ☐ physical presence or ☐ online notarization, this _____ (date) by _____ (name of officer or agent, title of officer or agent) of _____ (name of corporation acknowledging), a (state or place of incorporation) corporation, on behalf of the corporation. He/she is personally known to me or has produced (type of identification) as identification.

    _____ (Signature of Notary)   (Seal of Notary)

    _____ (Name of Notary, printed, typed or stamped)

- Partnership Acknowledgment Short-Form Certificate — for a partner or partners acting on behalf of a partnership:

    State of Florida

    County of _____

The foregoing instrument was acknowledged before me by means of ☐ physical presence or ☐ online notarization, this _____ (date) by _____ (name of acknowledging partner or agent), partner (or agent) on behalf of _____ (name of partnership), a partnership. He/she is personally known to me or has produced _____ (type of identification) as identification.

- **Attorney in Fact Acknowledgment Short-Form Certificate —** for an attorney in fact acting on behalf of a principal:

    State of Florida

    County of _____

    The foregoing instrument was acknowledged before me by means of ☐ physical presence or ☐ online notarization, this _____ (date) by _____ (name of attorney in fact) as attorney in fact, who is personally known to me or who has produced _____ (type of identification) as identification on behalf of _____ (Name of principal).

    _____ (Signature of Notary)   (Seal of Notary)

    _____ (Name of Notary, printed, typed or stamped)

- **Representative Acknowledgment Short-Form Certificate —** for a public officer, trustee, executor, administrator, guardian or other representative acting on behalf of an entity or person:

    State of Florida

    County of _____

    The foregoing instrument was acknowledged before me by means of ☐ physical presence or ☐ online notarization, this _____ (date) by _____ (name and title of position), who is personally known to me or who has produced _____ (type of identification) as identification.

    _____ (Signature of Notary)   (Seal of Notary)

    _____ (Name of Notary, printed, typed or stamped)

Identification of Acknowledger. In an acknowledgment, the Notary must identify the signer either through personal knowledge, credible identifying witness(es) or identification documents (FS 117.05[5]). (See "Identifying Document Signers," pages 9–10.)

Witnessing Signature Not Required. For an acknowledgment, the document does not have to be signed in the Notary's presence. Rather, the document signer need only acknowledge having made the signature. The document could have been signed an hour before, a week before, a year before, etc. As long as the signer appears before the Notary at the time of notarization to acknowledge having signed, the Notary may execute the acknowledgment. (However, for a jurat notarization requiring an oath or affirmation, the document must be signed in the presence of the Notary. See "Jurats," pages 35–36.)

Out-of-State Acknowledgments. Acknowledgment certificates completed outside of Florida by Notaries of another state in accordance with the laws of that state may be recorded in Florida. However, acknowledgments completed in Florida for use out of the state must substantially comply with the wording prescribed in the Florida Statutes, Sections 117.05[13] or 695.25.

Terminology. In discussing the notarial act of acknowledgment, it is important to use the proper terminology. A Notary takes or executes an acknowledgment, while a document signer makes or gives an acknowledgment.

Who May Take. In addition to Notaries, the following officials may take acknowledgments within the state of Florida (FS 695.03):

1. A civil-law Notary of Florida.
2. A judge, clerk or deputy clerk of any court.
3. A United States commissioner or magistrate.

Outside of Florida, but within the United States and its jurisdictions, acknowledgments may be executed by (FS 695.03):

1. A Notary Public of the state or jurisdiction.
2. A Florida civil law Notary or a commissioner of deeds appointed by the Florida governor.

3. A judge or clerk of any court of the United States, or of any state, territory or district.

4. A U.S. commissioner or magistrate.

5. A justice of the peace, master in chancery or registrar or recorder of deeds in any state, territory or district having a seal.

Outside of United States jurisdictions, acknowledgments may be executed by (FS 695.03):

1. A Notary Public of the foreign jurisdiction.

2. A Florida civil-law Notary or a commissioner of deeds appointed by the Florida Governor.

3. An ambassador, envoy, minister, commissioner, charge d'affaires, consul general, consul, vice consul, consular agent or other U.S. consular officer in the foreign jurisdiction.

4. A U.S. military or naval officer authorized to perform the duties of a Notary Public.

Certified Copies

Purpose. Florida Notaries have the authority to certify — or "attest" — that a copy of an original document is a complete and true reproduction of the document that was copied. The Notary's authority to certify copies is limited to documents that are not vital records or public records, if a copy can be made by the custodian of the public record (FS 117.05[12][a]).

Procedure. The permanent custodian of the original document must present it to the Notary and request a certified copy. The Notary must make or closely supervise the making of the photocopy to ensure that it is true, exact and unaltered (FS 117.05[12][a]).

Examples of the documents that may be lawfully photocopied and certified by a Florida Notary are: a diploma, a Florida driver's license, a vehicle title, a Social Security card, a medical record, a passport, a bill of sale, a contract or a lease.

Precautions. Florida law permits Notaries to certify only photocopies of original documents, never hand-rendered reproductions. To minimize the opportunity for fraud, the making of the photocopy should be done by the Notary. Otherwise, the Notary should carefully compare the copy to the original, word for word, to ensure that it is complete and identical.

Copy Certification of Recordable Documents Prohibited. Florida Notaries are prohibited from certifying copies of recordable documents. An individual who needs a certified copy of a recordable document such as a deed should first record the document and then have the recording agency provide a certified copy. A notary public may supervise the making of a copy of a tangible or an electronic record or the printing of an electronic record and attest to the trueness of the copy or of the printout, provided the document is neither a vital record in this state, another state, a territory of the United States, or another country, nor a public record, if a copy can be made by the custodian of the public record (FS 117.05[12][a]).

Copy Certification of Vital Records Prohibited. Florida Notaries are expressly prohibited from certifying copies of birth or death certificates, because these are vital records. Only officials in a bureau of vital statistics or other public record office may certify originals or copies of such certificates. A Notary's "certification" of such a copy may lend credibility to what is actually a counterfeit or altered document (FS 117.05[12] [a]).

Certified Copy Certificate. Attesting to the trueness of a copy should substantially comply with the following (FS 117.05[12][c]):

State of Florida

County of _____

On this the _____ day of _____ (month), _____ (year), I attest that the preceding or attached document is a true, exact, complete and unaltered photocopy made by me of _____ (copy of a tangible or an electronic record presented to me by the document's custodian), or a _____ (printout made by me from such record). If a printout, I further attest that, at the time of printing, no security features, if any, present on the electronic record, indicated that the record had been altered since execution.

_____ (Signature of Notary Public - State of Florida)

_____ (Print, Type, or Stamp Commissioned Name of Notary Public)

Copies of Notary Records

Written Request. If an individual desires a copy of a journal entry or other Notary record, it is recommended that the Notary require a written and signed request that specifies the name(s) of the party(ies) whose signature(s) was/were notarized, the type of document and the month and year of the notarization.

Inventorying a Safe-Deposit Box

Purpose. Florida law allows financial institutions, such as banks, to open a safe-deposit box if the rental fees are overdue, attempts have been made to notify the renter and no response has been received. A Notary Public is required to be present for the opening, to inventory the contents of the box and to complete a certificate as evidence (FS 655.94[1]).

Procedure. Both a Notary and an officer of the institution must be present at the time the safe-deposit box is opened. When the box is opened, the Notary must inventory the contents of the box and complete a certificate detailing the items discovered (FS 655.94[1]).

Journal Signature. If the Notary keeps a journal of notarial acts, it is recommended that the Notary obtain the signature of the officer and any witnesses as well.

Certificate for Inventorying a Safe-Deposit Box. The Notary's certificate should include the name of the lessee, the date of opening and a list of the contents. A copy of the certificate should be given to the institution, and the original should be placed in the package containing the contents (FS 655.94[1]).

Florida law does not provide specific wording for the certificate. The following form is suggested:

State of Florida

County of _____

On the _____ day of _____ (month), _____ (year), safe-deposit box number _____, rented in the name of _____, was opened by _____ (name of financial institution) in my presence and in the presence of _____ (name of officer). The contents of the box consisted of the following:

(list of contents)

_____ (Signature of bank officer)

_____ (Print or type name)

_____ (Signature of person opening box)

_____ (Print or type name)

_____ (Signature of Notary)   (Seal of Notary)

_____ (Name of Notary, printed, typed or stamped)

Jurats

Part of Verification. In notarizing affidavits, depositions and other forms of written verification requiring an oath by the signer, the Notary normally executes a jurat.

Purpose. While the purpose of an acknowledgment is to positively identify a document signer, the purpose of a verification with jurat is to compel truthfulness by appealing to the signer's conscience and fear of criminal penalties for perjury.

In executing a jurat, a Notary certifies that (FS 117.05):

1. The signer *personally appeared* before the Notary by physical presence or by means of audio-video communication technolog at the time of notarization on the date and in the county indicated (notarization based upon a telephone call or on familiarity with a signature is not acceptable).

2. The signer was *positively identified* by the Notary through either personal knowledge or satisfactory evidence. (See "Identifying Document Signers," pages 9–10.)

3. The Notary *witnessed the signature* being made at the time of notarization.
4. The Notary *administered an oath (or affirmation)* to the signer.

Certificate for a Jurat. A jurat is the wording, "Subscribed and sworn to (or affirmed) before me by means of ☐ physical presence or ☐ online notarization on this (date) by (name of signer) …" or similar language. The following wording is prescribed by Florida law (FS 117.05[13][a]):

> State of Florida
> County of _____
>
> Sworn to (or affirmed) and subscribed before me by means of ☐ physical presence or ☐ online notarization, this _____ day of _____ (month), _____(year), by _____ (name of signer).
>
> _____ (Signature of Notary)   (Seal of Notary)
> _____ (Name of Notary, printed, typed or stamped)
> Personally known _____ OR produced identification _____
> Type of identification produced _____

Wording for Jurat Oath (Affirmation). If not otherwise prescribed, a Florida Notary may use the following or similar wording to administer an oath (or affirmation) with a jurat:

> Do you solemnly swear that the statements in this document are true to the best of your knowledge and belief, so help you God?
>
> (Do you solemnly affirm that the statements in this document are true to the best of your knowledge and belief?)

Marriages

Authority. Florida is one of only a few U.S. states that allow Notaries to perform marriages. Maine, Nevada, South Carolina and one parish in Louisiana are the others. Unless the Notary is also a clergy member, the Notary-performed marriage is a civil ceremony (FS 117.045 and 741.07[1]).

Procedure. The Notary must ensure that the couple present a valid marriage license from a county court judge or clerk of the circuit court. The Notary may then perform the ceremony within the boundaries of the state (web, FAQ's).

Certificate for Marriage. The Notary is responsible for completing the certificate on the appropriate portion of the marriage license. The Notary must then return the license to the office of the county court judge or clerk of the circuit court that issued the license within 10 days after the marriage is performed (FS 741.08).

Relatives. Notaries may perform marriage ceremonies for relatives. The statute prohibiting notarizing for a son, daughter, mother or father does not apply to this situation because the Notary is not notarizing the signature of the bride and groom. He or she is merely certifying that the couple has been joined in matrimony according to Florida law (1991 Florida Attorney General's Opinion 91-70).

Fees. For solemnizing the rites of matrimony, a Notary Public may charge the same fee that clerks of the circuit court can charge for like services: $30 (FS 117.045 and 28.24[29]).

Oaths and Affirmations

Purpose. An oath is a solemn, spoken pledge to a Supreme Being. An affirmation is a solemn, spoken pledge on one's own personal honor, with no reference to a Supreme Being. Both are usually promises of truthfulness and have the same legal effect.

In taking an oath or affirmation in an official proceeding, a person may be subject to criminal penalties for perjury should he or she fail to be truthful.

An oath or affirmation can be a full-fledged notarial act in its own right, as when giving an oath of office to a public official (when "swearing in" a public official), or it can be part of the process of notarizing a document (e.g., executing a jurat or swearing in a subscribing witness).

A person who objects to taking an oath may instead be given an affirmation.

Power to Administer. Florida Notaries and certain other officers are authorized to administer and complete certificates for oaths and affirmations (FS 117.03).

An acknowledgment is not an acceptable substitution for an oath. A Notary may not take an acknowledgment in lieu of an oath if an oath is required (FS 117.03).

Wording for Oath (Affirmation). If law does not dictate otherwise, a Florida Notary may use the following or similar words in administering an oath (or affirmation):

- Oath (Affirmation) for affiant signing an affidavit:

    Do you solemnly swear that the statements in this document are true to the best of your knowledge and belief, so help you God?

    (Do you solemnly affirm that the statements in this document are true to the best of your knowledge and belief?)

- Oath (Affirmation) for witness testifying in a court case:

    Do you solemnly swear that the evidence you shall give in this issue (or matter), pending between (first party) and (second party), shall be the truth, the whole truth and nothing but the truth, so help you God?

    (Do you solemnly affirm that the evidence you shall give in this issue [or matter], pending between [first party] and [second party], shall be the truth, the whole truth and nothing but the truth?)

- Oath (Affirmation) for credible identifying witness:

    Do you solemnly swear that (person making the acknowledgment) is the person named in the document; that (person making the acknowledgment) is personally known to you; that it is your reasonable belief that the circumstances of (person making the acknowledgment) are such that it would be very difficult or impossible for him/her to obtain another form of identification; that (person making the acknowledgment) does not possess any of the acceptable identification documents; and that you do not have a financial interest nor are you named in the document being acknowledged, so help you God?

    (Do you solemnly affirm that [person making the acknowledgment] is the person named in the document; that [person making the acknowledgment] is personally known to you; that it is your reasonable belief that the circumstances of [person making the acknowledgment] are such that it would be very difficult or impossible for him/her to obtain another form of identification; that [person making the acknowledgment] does not possess any of the acceptable identification documents; and that you do not have a financial interest nor are you named in the document being acknowledged?)

In addition to administering the oath or affirmation to a credible identifying witness, the Notary must obtain a sworn, written statement from that witness. (See pages 12–15.)

Response Required. The oath or affirmation wording must be spoken aloud, and the person taking the oath or affirmation must answer affirmatively with, "I do," "Yes" or the like. A nod or grunt is not a clear and sufficient response. If a person is unable to speak, the Notary may rely upon written notes to communicate.

Ceremony and Gestures. To impress upon the oath-taker or affirmant the importance of truthfulness, the Notary is encouraged to lend a sense of ceremony and formality to the oath or affirmation. During the administration of an oath or affirmation, the Notary and oath-taker or affirmant may traditionally raise their right hands, though this is not a legal requirement. Notaries generally have discretion to use words and gestures they feel will most compellingly appeal to the conscience of the oath-taker or affirmant.

Affidavits

Purpose. An affidavit is a signed statement made under oath or affirmation by a person called an affiant, and it is used for a variety of purposes, both in and out of court.

Affidavits are used to make sworn statements for many reasons, from declaring losses to an insurance company to declaring U.S. citizenship before traveling to a foreign country. An affidavit is a document containing a statement voluntarily signed and sworn to or affirmed before a Notary or other official with oath administering powers. If used in a judicial proceeding, only one side in the case need participate in the affidavit process, in contrast to the deposition.

Procedure. For an affidavit, the Notary must administer an oath or affirmation and complete some form of jurat, which the Notary signs and seals.

In an affidavit, the Notary's certificate typically sandwiches the affiant's signed statement, with the venue and affiant's name at the top of the document and the jurat wording at the end. The Notary is responsible for the venue, affiant's name and any Notary text at the beginning and end of the affidavit. The affiant is responsible for the signed statement in the middle.

Certificate for Affidavits. Affidavits typically require jurat certificates. (See "Jurats," pages 35–36.)

Oath (Affirmation) for Affidavits. If no other wording is prescribed, a Notary may use the following language in administering an oath (affirmation) for an affidavit or deposition:

> Do you solemnly swear that the statements made in this affidavit are the truth, the whole truth, and nothing but the truth, so help you God?

> (Do you solemnly affirm that the statements made in this affidavit are the truth, the whole truth, and nothing but the truth?)

Response Required. For an oath or affirmation, the affiant must respond aloud and affirmatively, with "I do," "Yes" or the like.

Depositions

Purpose. A deposition is a signed transcript of the signer's oral statements taken down for use in a judicial proceeding. This deposition signer is called the deponent.

With a deposition, both sides in a lawsuit or court case have the opportunity to cross-examine the deponent. Questions and answers are transcribed into a written statement. Used only in judicial proceedings, a deposition is then signed and sworn to before an oath-administering official.

Procedure. Florida Notaries who are not licensed attorneys do not have the power to take depositions. This duty is most often executed by trained and certified shorthand reporters, also known as court reporters. Notaries may administer the oath or affirmation to the deponent only (Governor's Reference Manual, p. 13).

For a deposition, the Notary typically administers an oath or affirmation and completes some form of jurat, which he or she signs and seals.

Certificate for Depositions. To administer an oath or affirmation to the deponent, the Notary uses a jurat certificate:

> State of Florida
> County of _____
>
> In my capacity as a Notary Public of the State of Florida, I certify that on the _____ day of _____ (month), _____ (year), at _____ (time) a.m./p.m., _____ (name of deponent) personally appeared before me and took an oath (or affirmation) for the purpose of giving testimony in the matter: .
>
> _____ (Signature of Notary) (Seal of Notary)
> _____ (Name of Notary, printed, typed or stamped)
> Personally known _____ OR produced identification _____
> Type of identification produced _____

Oath (Affirmation) for Depositions. If no other wording is prescribed, a Notary may use the following language in administering an oath (affirmation) for an affidavit or deposition:

> Do you solemnly swear that the statements made in this deposition are the truth, the whole truth and nothing but the truth, so help you God?
>
> (Do you solemnly affirm that the statements made in this deposition are the truth, the whole truth and nothing but the truth?)

Response Required. For an oath or affirmation, the affiant must respond aloud and affirmatively, with "I do," "Yes" or the like.

Verifying a Vehicle Identification Number

Purpose. When a person applies for a Florida title on a used motor vehicle, a physical inspection must be done by an individual authorized to certify a vehicle identification number (VIN). Florida law authorizes a Notary to make such a certification. The owner of the vehicle must swear before a Notary that the VIN and odometer reading are correct (FS 319.23[3][a][2]).

State officials explain that the Florida Department of Highway Safety and Motor Vehicles has issued new title forms to be used for new vehicles. These new forms do not require notarization, and the Department has omitted the Notary wording from the form. However, older title forms which do require notarization are still in circulation on older and used vehicles. Therefore, the Notary should be aware of the differences and understand how to notarize the older forms if presented by a signer.

Verification Form. Both the owner's declaration and the Notary's verification are included on a form provided by the Department of Highway Safety and Motor Vehicles.

Part A of the form is used for the owner's sworn statement pertaining to the VIN and odometer reading. Part B of the form requires the Notary to perform a physical inspection of the vehicle for the purpose of verifying that the vehicle's identification number is the same as the number on the form. This part of the form must also be signed, sealed and dated by the Notary (2016 RMN, p. 17).

Fees for Notary Services

Maximum Fees. The following maximum fees for performing notarial acts are allowed by Florida law (FS 28.24[29], 117.045 and 117.05[2]):

- **Acknowledgments — $10.** For taking an acknowledgment, the fee is not to exceed $10 for each certificate. For notarizing a document with three signatures, a maximum of $10 may be charged. However, if three certificates are used for the same notarization, then $30 may be charged.

- **Certified Copy — $10.** A maximum of $10 per copy may be charged by a Notary for providing a certified copy.

- **Taking Inventory of a Safe-Deposit Box — $10.** For being present at the opening of a safe-deposit box and completing the certificate, the maximum fee is $10.

- **Jurats — $10.** For executing a jurat, including the administration of the oath or affirmation, the fee is not to exceed $10 per certificate.

- **Marriages — $30.** For solemnizing the rites of matrimony, the Notary may not charge more than $30.

- **Oaths and Affirmations — $10.** For administering an oath or affirmation, with or without completion of a jurat, the fee is not to exceed $10 per person.

- **Verifying a Vehicle Identification Number — $10.** For notarization of Part B, the fee is $10.

- **Online Notarizations — $25.** For performing an online act, the fee is not to exceed $25.

Option Not to Charge. Notaries are not required to charge for their Notary services, and they may charge any fee less than the maximum.

Overcharging. Charging more than the legally prescribed fees is reason for the Governor to suspend a Notary's commission (FS 117.01[4][i]).

Travel Fees. Charges for travel by a Notary are not specified by law. Such fees should be charged only if the Notary and signer agree beforehand on the amount to be charged. The signer should understand that a travel fee is not stipulated by law and is a private arrangement separate from the authorized Notary fees described above.

Absentee Ballots. A Notary may not charge a fee for witnessing an absentee ballot in an election, but must witness the ballot if so requested by a voter (FS 117.05[2][b]).

Unauthorized Notary Practices

Proofs of Execution by Subscribing Witness. Although Florida statutes address the recording of documents proved by subscribing witness, the Florida Governor's office states that a proof of execution by subscribing witness is not a notarial act (FS 695.03 and web, FAQ's).

Notary Named in Document. A Notary Public may not notarize a document in which the Notary's name appears as a party to the transaction (FS 117.107[12]).

Blank Certificates. A Notary may not sign and affix a seal to a blank Notary certificate and then deliver that certificate to another person for the purpose of notarization (FS 117.107[3]).

Certifying Copies of Vital or Public Records. A Notary is not authorized to certify a copy of a document that is a vital or public record (FS 117.05[12][a]).

Incomplete Documents. It is unlawful to notarize an incomplete document. This does not apply to a blank endorsement or assignment of a negotiable or nonnegotiable note, or of a document given as security for such a note (FS 117.107[10]).

Mentally Incapable of Understanding. A Notary may not notarize for a person who appears "mentally incapable of understanding" the document's effect (FS 117.107[5]), or for a person that the Notary knows has been ruled mentally incapacitated by a court (FS 117.107[4]).

Notary's Own Signature. A Notary is not permitted to notarize his or her own signature (FS 117.107[12]).

Notarization Without Appearance. A Notary may not notarize the signature of a person who does not personally appear before the Notary at the time of notarization. A Notary who violates this law is guilty of a civil infraction and can be fined up to $5,000 regardless of whether the Notary had fraudulent intentions (FS 117.107[9]).

Notarizing for Relatives. A Notary may not notarize for a spouse, son, daughter, mother or father (FS 117.107[11]).

Signing False Names. A Notary may not sign a Notary certificate using any name other than the one under which he or she was commissioned (FS 117.107[1]). ■

Recordkeeping

Journal of Notarial Acts

Requirements and Recommendations. Although in the state of Florida, a journal is only required by law for online notarizations, both the National Notary Association and the Notary Section of the Governor's office recommend that every Notary keep a detailed, accurate and sequential journal of notarial acts even though it is not required by law (2016 RMN, p. 12).

A journal record of a transaction demonstrates that the Notary used reasonable care in identifying a document signer. Failure to keep a journal, while not unlawful, can cause problems for a Notary if a transaction is challenged for any reason. A permanently bound recordbook (not loose-leaf) with numbered pages and entry spaces is best for preserving the sequence of notarial acts and for protecting against unauthorized removal of pages or tampering.

Journal Entries. For each notarization, the following vital information should be recorded:

1. The date, time of day, and type of notarization (e.g., jurat, acknowledgment, etc.).

2. The date and type of document notarized (e.g., deed of trust, affidavit of support, etc.).

3. The printed name, address and the signature of each person

whose signature is notarized; the signature of any credible witness; and the signature of any witnesses to a signature by mark.

4. A statement as to how the signer's identity was confirmed. If by personal knowledge, the journal entry should read "Personal Knowledge." If by satisfactory evidence, the journal entry should contain either: a description of the ID card accepted, including the type of ID, the government agency issuing the ID, the serial or identifying number and the date of issuance or expiration; or the signature of each credible identifying witness and how the credible identifying witness was identified. (See "Credible Identifying Witness[es]," pages 12–15.)

5. The fee charged for the Notary service.

Additional Entries. Notaries may include additional information in the journal that is pertinent to a given notarization. Many Notaries, for example, enter the telephone number of all signers and witnesses, as well as the address where the notarization was performed, if not at the Notary's office. A description of the document signer's demeanor (e.g., "The signer appeared very nervous") or notations about the identity of other persons who were present for the notarization may also be included.

One important entry to include is the signer's representative capacity — whether the signer is acting as attorney in fact, trustee, guardian, corporate officer or in another capacity — if not signing on his or her own behalf.

Required Electronic Journal Entries. Journal requirements for electronic notarizations can be found in the Electronic and Online Notarization chapter of this *Primer*.

Journal Thumbprint. Many Notaries are asking document signers to leave a thumbprint in the journal. The journal thumbprint protects the Notary against claims that a signer did not appear and is a strong deterrent to forgery, because it represents absolute proof of the signer's identity and appearance before the Notary.

Provided the signer is willing, nothing prevents a Notary from asking for a thumbprint for every notarial act. Since a thumbprint is not required by law, however, the Notary may not refuse to notarize if the signer declines to leave one.

Journal-Entry Copies. A Notary's official journal is a public record. Accordingly, if any person submits a written request specifying the month and year of a particular notarization, as well as the type of document and the names of the signers, the Notary may provide that person with a photocopy of the particular entry in the journal — but of no other entries! Adjacent entries should be covered by a sheet of blank paper before the photocopy is made. (See "Copies of Notary Records," page 34.)

Never Surrender Journal. Notaries should never surrender control of their journals to anyone, unless subpoenaed by a court order. Even when an employer has paid for the Notary's journal and seal, they go with the Notary upon termination of employment; no person but the Notary can lawfully possess and use these official adjuncts of office (FS 117.05[3][d]).

Reasonable Care

Responsibility. As public servants, Notaries must act responsibly and exercise reasonable care in the performance of their official duties. If a Notary fails to do so, he or she may be subject to a civil suit to recover financial damages caused by the Notary's error or omission. In general, reasonable care is that degree of concern and attentiveness that a person of normal intelligence and responsibility would exhibit. If a Notary can show a judge or jury that he or she did everything expected of a reasonable person, the judge or jury is obligated by law to find the Notary not liable for damages.

Complying with all pertinent laws is the first rule of reasonable care for a Notary. If there are no statutory guidelines in a given instance, the Notary should "bend over backwards" to use common sense and prudence. ■

Notary Certificate and Seal

Notary Certificate

Requirement. In notarizing any document, a Notary must complete a Notary certificate. The certificate is wording that indicates exactly what the Notary has certified. The Notary certificate may either be on the document itself or on an attachment to it. The certificate should contain (FS 117.05[4]):

1. A *venue* indicating where the notarization is being performed. "State of Florida, County of _____," is the typical venue wording, with the county name inserted in the blank. The letters "SS." or "SCT." sometimes appear after the venue; they abbreviate the traditional Latin word scilicet, meaning "in particular" or "namely."

2. A *statement of particulars* which indicates what the notarization has attested to. An acknowledgment certificate would include such wording as: "On _____ (date) before me, _____ (name of Notary), personally appeared, _____ (name of signer), personally known to me (or proved to me on the basis of satisfactory evidence) to be the person(s) … etc." A jurat certificate would include such wording as: "Subscribed and sworn to (or affirmed) before me this _____ (date) by _____ (name of signer)."

3. A *testimonium clause*, which may be optional if the date is included in the statement of particulars: "Witness my hand and official seal, this the _____ day of _____ (month), _____ (year)." In this short sentence, the Notary formally attests to the truthfulness of the preceding facts in the certificate. "Hand" means signature.

4. The *official signature of the Notary*, exactly as the name appears on the commissioning paper. A facsimile signature stamp may not be used unless the Notary has a physical disability that prevents or limits signing and the Department of State is notified in writing and given a sample facsimile (FS 117.107[2]).

5. The *official seal of the Notary*. On many certificates the letters "L.S." appear, indicating where the seal is to be located.

In addition to the basic elements described above, acknowledgment and jurat certificates must also indicate the following (FS 117.05[4]):

- That the signer personally appeared before the Notary at the time of notarization.

- The exact date of the notarial act.

- The name of the person whose signature is being notarized.

- The manner in which the signer was identified.

- Print, type or stamp name of Notary below signature

Certificate Forms. When certificate wording is not preprinted on the document, a certificate form may be attached by the Notary. This form is typically stapled to the document's left margin following the signature page.

To prevent a certificate from being removed and fraudulently placed on another document, there are precautions a Notary can take. The Notary can write a brief description of the document on the certificate: "This certificate is attached to a _____ (title or type of document), _____ dated (date), of _____ (number) pages, signed by _____ (name[s] of signer[s])." The Notary also can note on the document that a certificate is attached: "See attached notarial certificate, dated (date) and certifying the signature(s) of (name[s] of signer[s])."

While fraud-deterrent steps such as these can make it much more difficult for a certificate form to be removed and misused, there is no absolute protection against its removal and misuse. Notaries must absolutely ensure that while a certificate remains in their control, it is attached only to its intended document.

Do Not Pre-Sign or Pre-Seal Certificates. A Notary should never sign and/or seal certificate forms ahead of time or permit other persons to attach Notary certificate forms to documents. Nor should the Notary send an unattached, signed, and sealed certificate forms through the mail — blank or completed — even if requested to do so by a signer who previously appeared before the Notary. These actions are prohibited by Florida law because they may facilitate fraud or forgery, and they could subject the Notary to lawsuits to recover damages resulting from the Notary's neglect or misconduct (FS 117.107[3]).

Correcting Certificates. A Notary may not change anything in a Notary certificate after the notarization is complete. State officials consider a notarization "complete" after the signer leaves the presence of the Notary after having a document notarized (FS 117.107[7-8]).

If a document and the incorrect — or incomplete — certificate are returned to the Notary, the Notary should treat the transaction as a new notarization; the signer must again personally appear and be identified by the Notary. A note should be made on the original Notary certificate saying that the document has been notarized again due to an error in the original certificate. Likewise, the new Notary certificate should have a notation stating the same.

For additional information or for questions regarding specific situations, contact the Governor's Notary Section at (850) 717-0310.

False Certificate. A Notary who knowingly completes a false Notary certificate is guilty of a felony of the third degree and subject to criminal penalties. A Notary would be completing a false certificate, for example, if he or she signed and sealed an acknowledgment certificate indicating that a signer personally appeared when the signer actually did not (FS 117.105).

Notary Seal

Requirement. A Florida Notary must affix an impression of an official seal on the certificate portion of every document notarized (FS 117.05[3]).

Inking Seal. For paper documents, the official seal of office is a rubber stamp inking seal. The seal must imprint a photographically reproducible impression in black ink (FS 117.05[3][a]).

An embosser may be used in addition to the required photographically reproducible seal, but not in place of it. The embosser must not be used over the ink seal or over the Notary's signature (FS 117.05[3][a]).

Format. Florida law does not designate a particular size or shape for the official seal. Typical inking seals are rectangular and about one inch wide by two and one-half inches long.

Required Information. The seal impression must clearly show the following information (FS 117.05[3][a]):

- Name of the Notary (exactly as it appears on the commission certificate).

- The words "Notary Public — State of Florida."

- The Notary's commission expiration date.

- The Notary's commission number.

The seal may contain any additional information — such as the name of the Notary's bonding company — or emblems, except for the Great Seal of the State of Florida (2016 RMN, p. 9).

Lost or Misplaced Seal. A Notary whose seal is lost, misplaced or believed to be in someone else's possession, must immediately notify the Department of State in writing (FS 117.05[3][c]).

Possession of Seal. Any person who unlawfully possesses a

Notary Public's seal or any papers relating to notarial acts is guilty of a misdemeanor of the second degree (FS 117.05[3][d]).

Placement of Seal Impression. The Notary's official seal impression should be placed near his or her signature on the Notary certificate. It must be easily readable and should not be placed over signatures or any printed matter on the document. An illegible or improperly placed seal may result in rejection of the document by a recorder (FS 117.05[4][i]).

L.S. The letters "L.S." — from the Latin *locus sigilli*, meaning "location of the seal" — appear on many notarial certificates to indicate where the Notary seal should be placed. Only an embosser seal, used optionally in addition to an inking seal, should be placed over these letters. The inking seal should be placed near but not over the letters.

In-Person Electronic Notarization and Remote Online Notarization

In-Person Electronic Notarization

Electronic Notarization Defined. Florida law defines an electronic notarial act as an official notarial act using electronic documents and electronic signatures.

Authorization. According to Florida law, any document requiring notarization may be notarized electronically.

Procedure. In-person electronic notarization, also called IPEN or eNotarization, still requires the Notary and signer to meet face-to-face and be physically in the same room. Like pen and paper notarizations, the Notary must identify the signer through personal knowledge or satisfactory evidence, screen the signer for willingness and awareness, and certify the facts for the requested notarization. However, for electronic notarizations, the document is presented electronically, such as on a computer or tablet, and the signature will be affixed electronically by the signer. The Notary certificate will be provided at the end of the document or logically attached to the document for the Notary to complete and affix the electronic signature and the electronic seal.

Electronic Signature Requirements. The Notary's electronic signature must be (FS 117.021[1] and [2]):

- Unique to the Notary;

- Capable of independent verification;

- Retained under the Notary's sole control and include access protection using passwords or codes under control of the Notary; and

- Attached to or logically associated with the electronic document in a manner that any subsequent alteration to the electronic document displays evidence of the alteration.

The electronic signature and seal information may be affixed by either a public key certificate or by an electronic notary system issued at the third or higher level of assurance as defined by the U.S. National Institute of Standards and Technology (NIST).

Physical Seal Not Required. An electronic seal is not required when the electronic signature of the Notary contains the following (FS 117.021[3]):

- The full name of the Notary exactly as provided on the Notary's commission application;

- The words 'Notary Public State of Florida';

- The Notary's commission expiration date; and

- The Notary's commission number (FS 117.021[3]).

Technology. A Notary may select the technology to be used for electronic notarizations. Signers cannot require the Notary to use a particular technology. However, a Notary's contract or employer may require the use of a specific technology system (FS 117.021[4]).

Remote Online Notarization

Purpose. When the Notary and signer cannot meet face-to-face in the same room, a remote online notarization, also referred to as RON, can be performed.

Remote Online Notarization Defined. Florida defines online notarization as the performance of a notarial act using electronic means in which the principal or any witness appears before the Notary by means of audio-video communication technology.

Registration Required. In order to become an online Notary, an applicant must have an existing commission as a traditional Notary, civil law Notary or commissioner of deeds.

Course Required. An online Notary applicant must complete a two-hour remote online notary training course, pass an exam and receive a completion certificate.

Contract with a Technology Service Provider. To apply to be an online Notary, you must first have a contract with a company that will provide the technological support needed to perform online notarizations.

The Florida Department of State does not recommend nor endorse any third-party vendors. The basic requirements for vendors' technology are found under Chapter 117, Florida Statutes, and Chapter 1N-7001, Florida Administrative Register.

Bond. An online Notary applicant must purchase $25,000 bond. If the Notary's bond already meets those requirements, it is not necessary to purchase separate or additional coverage. Florida Notaries who already have a $7,500 surety bond for their traditional Notary commissions must increase the bond to $25,000 to apply to be remote Notaries.

Errors and Omissions Insurance. Although errors and omissions insurance is not mandatory for traditional commissions, the state does require online Notaries to purchase a $25,000 errors and omissions policy. Notaries who currently have an insurance policy, should check with the insurer to determine if it meets Florida RON requirements.

Application Submission. The application can be found on the Department of State's website. It must be printed, completed, notarized and submitted to the Florida Department of State with the following:

- Online Notary application
- A copy of current Florida Notary commission appointment
- Evidence of completing online Notary training
- Evidence of obtaining a $25,000 bond
- Evidence of $25,000 errors and omissions insurance policy
- Application Fee of $10

Procedure. Remote Online Notarization requires the Notary and signer to meet via audio-video technology that allows them to see and hear each other in real-time. The electronic record or document and the electronic Notary certificate are uploaded to a shared platform by a Notary technology provider, and the notarization takes place via that platform. The Notary would still follow the fundamental steps for the notarization. The Notary screens the signer for identity, willingness and awareness and certifies the facts for the requested notarization. Then the Notary completes the electronic certificate and affixes an electronic signature and seal. An electronic journal record is made, along with an audio-video recording of the transaction.

Location of Notary and Signer. The Notary must be located within the state of Florida at the time of the remote online notarization. However, the signer is not required to be within the state of Florida at the time of notarization (FS 117.209[3]).

Identification of the Remotely Located Signer. Verifying the signer's identity remains one of the most important roles of the Notary. A Notary must determine identity of the remotely located individual through personal knowledge or all the following:

1. Remote presentation of a government-issued identification credential.

2. Credential analysis of each government-issued identification credential (see Credential Analysis, page 57).

3. Identity proofing of each principal in the form of knowledge-based authentication or another method of identity proofing that conforms to state standards (see Identity Proofing below).

Credential Analysis is the process by which the government-issued identification card of the principal is validated. The process requires a third party to use technology confirming the security features on an ID and that the ID is not fraudulent through a review of public or proprietary data sources.

Knowledge Based Authentication is a method of identity proofing which seeks to prove the identity of someone. It is a set of questions which pertain to an individual and are formulated from public or proprietary data sources. The principal must answer at least 80% of the questions correct within a two-minute time constraint (FS 117.295[3][a]).

Certificate of Remote Notarial Act. As with traditional notarizations, the Notary must compete sign and seal a Notary certificate for each transaction. The certificate must include a notation that the notarization is an online notarization, which may be satisfied by placing the term "Online Notary" in or adjacent to the Notary's seal (FS 117.265[7]).

To complete the notarization, the Notary must provide a tamper-evident electronic signature to the Notary certificate and affix an electronic Notary seal (FAC 1N-7.001[7]).

Electronic Journal. An online Notary must keep, maintain and keep secure an electronic journal of all online notarizations performed. The electronic journal must include the following information:

- The date and time of the notarization.

- The type of notarial act performed, whether an oath or acknowledgment.

- The type, the title, or a description of the electronic record or proceeding.

- The name and address of each principal involved in the transaction or proceeding.
- Evidence of identity of each principal involved in the transaction or proceeding in either of the following forms:
    1. A statement that the person is personally known to the online notary public; or
    2. A notation of the type of government-issued identification credential provided to the online Notary with an indication that the government-issued identification credential satisfied the credential analysis; and an indication that the principal satisfactorily passed the identity proofing.
- The fee, if any, charged for the notarization (FS 117.245[1]).

Backup of Electronic Journal. An online Notary must take reasonable steps to maintain a backup record of the electronic journal (FS 117.245[3][b]).

Audio Video Recording. In addition to the electronic journal, an audio video recording of the entire remote online notarization must be made. The service provider must retain an uninterrupted and unedited copy of the online notarization recording.

The Notary must ensure that the recording includes all the following:

1. Appearance by the principal and any witness before the Notary.
2. Confirmation of the identity of the principal and any witness.
3. A general description or identification of the records to be signed.
4. At the commencement of the recording, recitation by the Notary of information sufficient to identify the notarial act.
5. A declaration by the principal that his or her signature on the record is knowingly and voluntarily made.

6. All the actions and spoken words of the principal, Notary, and any required witness during the entire online notarization, including the signing of any records before the Notary (FS 117.245[2]).

Security of Journal and Recordings. The journal must be kept under the control of the Notary and may not be used by other Notaries, other than a remote online notarization service provider or other authorized person providing services to an online Notary to facilitate performance of online notarizations (FS 117.255[1][b]).

Retention of Electronic Journal and Recordings. The electronic journal and the audio-video recordings must be maintained for at least 10 years after the date of the notarial act (FS 117.245[4]).

Disposition of Journal. An online Notary, a guardian of an incapacitated online Notary, or a personal representative of a deceased online Notary may contract with and delegate a secure repository to retain the electronic journal. The Department of State must be notified of such delegation within 30 days, including the effective date of the delegation and the address and contact information for the repository. If an online Notary delegates to a repository, the Notary must make an entry in his or her electronic journal identifying the repository (FS 117.245[4]).

Disposition of Recordings. A service provider may delegate to a repository the duty to retain the required recordings of audio-video communications, provided that the Department of State is notified of such delegation within 30 days. The notification must include the effective date of the delegation and the address and contact information for the repository. The repository must fulfill the responsibilities of the online Notary service provider to provide copies or access under Florida law [FS] s. 117.255(2) and (3) (FS 117.245[4]).

Fees for Remote Online Notarization. A Notary may charge up to $25 for each remote online notarization.

Electronic Witnessing

Witnessing of Electronic Documents. As a part of the new online notarization law, Florida allows the witnessing of electronic documents using the same communication technology as for online notarizations. For example, witnesses to electronic wills or mortgages, may either be in the physical presence of the principal at the time of signing, or in a different location and sign the electronic documents using communication technology.

Witness Requirements. When witnessing an electronic document, the witness must either be in the physical presence of the principal or appear through audio-video communication technology at the time the principal affixes the electronic signature. The witness must hear the principal make a statement to the effect that the principal has signed the electronic document (FS 117.285[3]). The witness then signs the electronic document using communication technology.

If the witness is not in the presence of the principal, but appearing via audio-video communication, the principal and the witness must be identified with the procedures required for identifying a remotely located signer (see pages 56–57). If the witness is in the presence of the principal, the witness must state his or her name and current address during the audio-video recording (FS 117.285[2]).

Notary's Role in Electronic Witnessing. A Florida online Notary is authorized to supervise the witnessing of electronic documents using the same audio-video communication technology used for online notarization (FS 117.285). Supervising the witnessing of an electronic signature is a notarial act in Florida.

Legality and Limitations of Electronic Witnessing. Although electronic witnessing is a legal act, there are limitations when notarizing certain electronic documents — in particular, powers of attorney. The authority a principal can grant to an agent is limited when witnessed remotely (FS 709.2202) (FS 709.2202). Any legal questions about power of attorney limitations should be referred to an attorney. It is important to remember Notaries cannot give legal advice. Giving legal advice would be considered the unauthorized practice of law.

Specific Requirements for Certain Documents. When performing an electronic witnessing of a last will under FS 732, a revocable trust with testamentary aspects as described in FS 736.0403(2)(b), a health care directive, an agreement concerning succession or a waiver of spousal rights under FS 732.701 or 732.702, or a power of attorney authorizing any of the transactions enumerated in FS 709.2208 (FS 117.285[5] and fewer than two witnesses are in the physical presence of the principal, the online Notary must ask the principal to provide verbal answers to 5 questions in substantially the following form:

1. Are you currently married? If so, name your spouse.

2. Please state the names of anyone who assisted you in accessing this video conference today.

3. Please state the names of anyone who assisted you in preparing the documents you are signing today.

4. Where are you currently located?

5. Who is in the room with you?

The online Notary must consider the responses to these questions in carrying out the responsibility set forth in FS 117.107(5), which says, "A notary public may not notarize a signature on a document if it appears that the person is mentally incapable of understanding the nature and effect of the document at the time of notarization."

Responding to Legal Requests. A Notary or remote online notarization service provider must provide the following information in response to a subpoena, court order, authorized law enforcement inquiry or any other lawful request:

- The last known address of each witness who witnessed the signing of an electronic record using audio-video communication technology under this section.

- A principal's responses to the questions 1-5 above.

- An uninterrupted and unedited copy of the recording of the audio-video communication in which an online notarization is performed (FS 117.285[6]). ■

Misconduct, Fines and Penalties

Maintenance of Commission

Application Misstatement. Significant misstatement or omission in the application for a Notary commission is reason for the Governor to suspend a Notary's commission (FS 117.01[4][a]).

Commission Name. A person may not apply for a Notary commission in a name other than his or her legal name. A person applying for a commission must submit proof of identity to the Department of State upon request. A person who violates this provision is guilty of a felony of the third degree (FS 117.05[1]).

Falsely Acting as a Notary. Any person who willfully acts as a Notary while not lawfully commissioned is guilty of a misdemeanor in the second degree. Also guilty is a Notary who knowingly acts as such after his or her commission has expired (FS 117.05[7] and [8]).

Failure to Report Name or Address Change. A Notary who fails to report a change of name, address or telephone number is guilty of neglect of duty, and his or her commission may be suspended. This includes failure to request an amended commission after making such change (FS 117.01[4][g] and 117.05[9]).

Failure to Maintain Bond. Failure to maintain the required $7,500 bond as prescribed in the law is cause for the Governor to suspend the Notary's commission (FS 117.01[4][j]). (See "Notary Bond," pages 3–4.)

Commission Suspension. If the Notary receives notice from the Department of State that his or her office has been declared vacant or the commission has been suspended, the Notary shall immediately mail or deliver the commission to the Secretary of State and destroy the official Notary seal (FS 117.01[5]).

Illegal and Improper Acts

Official Misconduct. Commission of an act involving dishonesty, fraud or intentional violation of any Notary law is reason for the Governor to refuse to grant, revoke or suspend a Notary's commission (FS 117.01[4][d]).

Official misconduct comprises intent to benefit oneself or to cause harm to another, including knowingly falsifying or causing someone to falsify a document. Official misconduct is a felony in the third degree (FS 838.022).

Notarization Without Appearance. Notarizing the signature of a person who does not personally appear before the Notary at the time of notarization is an act of official misconduct. A Notary who violates the law regarding personal appearance is guilty of a civil infraction and can be fined up to $5,000, even if the Notary had no fraudulent intentions. A violator with intent to defraud is guilty of a felony in the third degree (FS 117.107[9]).

Notary's Own Signature. Notaries are not permitted to notarize their own signatures (FS 117.05[1]).

Beneficial Interest. A Notary Public may not notarize a document in which his or her name appears as a party to the transaction (FS 117.107[12]).

Notarizing for Relatives. The law specifically prohibits a Notary from notarizing for a spouse, son, daughter, mother or father of the Notary (FS 117.107[11]).

Mentally Incapacitated. If the Notary knows that the document signer has been judged mentally incapacitated and the notarization requires exercise of rights that have been removed pursuant to Florida Statutes, Section 744.3215(2) or (3), the Notary may not notarize (FS 117.107[4]).

Certifying Copies of Recordable Documents. A Notary is not authorized to certify a copy of a document that is a public record if a copy can be made by another public official (FS 117.05[12][a]).

A Notary also may not certify a document that is a vital record in Florida or any state or U.S. territory (FS 117.05[12]).

Incomplete Documents. It is unlawful for a Florida Notary to notarize a document that is not complete. This prohibition does not apply to a negotiable or nonnegotiable note, or to a document given as security for such a note (FS 117.107[10]).

Blank Certificates. A Notary may not sign and affix a seal to a blank Notary certificate and then deliver that certificate to another person for the purpose of notarization (FS 117.107[3]).

False Certificate. A Notary who knowingly completes a false notarial certificate or who falsely or fraudulently takes an acknowledgment is guilty of a felony in the third degree, which is punishable by a $5,000 fine or up to five years in jail. A Notary completes a false certificate, for example, if he or she signed and sealed an acknowledgment certificate indicating that a signer personally appeared when the signer actually did not (FS 117.105).

Signing False Names. A Notary may not sign a Notary certificate using any other name than the one under which he or she was commissioned (FS 117.107[1]).

Unlawful Possession. Any person who unlawfully possesses a Notary seal or any papers relating to notarial acts is guilty of a misdemeanor in the second degree. Such conviction is punishable by a fine of $500 or up to 60 days in jail (FS 117.05[3][d]).

False or Misleading Advertising. The use of false or misleading advertising by a Notary to represent that he or she has duties, rights and privileges not given by law is grounds for the Governor to suspend a Notary's commission (FS 117.01[4][e]).

This includes failing to include in a foreign language advertisement the statement, "I am not an attorney licensed to practice law in the state of Florida, and I may not give legal advice or accept fees for legal advice," or including a literal translation of the words "Notary Public" into a language other than English (FS 117.05[10] and [11]). (See "Advertising," pages 25–25.)

Unauthorized Practice of Law. The unauthorized practice of law, such as giving advice about a legal document when one is not a lawyer, is reason for the Governor to suspend a Notary's commission (FS 117.01[4][f]).

A Notary is not authorized to change anything in a written instrument after it has been signed by anyone (FS 117.107[7]). It is also considered the unauthorized practice of law for a Notary to take a deposition. Notaries may only administer an oath or affirmation to a deponent (FS 454.23).

Overcharging. Charging more than the legally prescribed fees is reason for the Governor to refuse to grant or to suspend a Notary's commission (FS 117.01[4][i]).

Misrepresentation. Commission of an act involving misrepresentation of authority or commission of fraud comprises neglect of duty and is grounds for suspension of the Notary's commission by the Governor (FS 117.01[4][h]).

Must Identify Signer. A Notary may not notarize a signature on a document unless the Notary personally knows, or has satisfactory evidence that the person is the one described in the document (FS 117.05[5]).

Facsimile of Notary's Signature. A Notary may not use a facsimile stamp to affix his or her official signature unless the Notary has a physical disability that limits his or her ability to sign his or her name. The Notary must submit written notice to the Department of State, along with a sample of the facsimile signature stamp (FS 117.107[2]).

Signer Doesn't Understand. A Notary may not notarize a document if it appears that the signer is mentally incapable of understanding the nature and significance of the document at the time of notarization (FS 117.107[5]).

Foreign-Language Documents and Signers. A Notary may not take the acknowledgment of a person who does not speak or understand the English language, unless the nature of the document to be notarized is translated into a language that the signer can understand (FS 117.107[6]).

Correcting Certificates. A Notary may not change anything in a Notary certificate once the notarization is complete. State officials consider a notarization "complete" when the signer leaves the presence of the Notary after having a document notarized (FS 117.107[8]). (See "Correcting Certificates," page 50.)

Seal Exclusive Property. The official Notary seal is the exclusive property of the Notary named on it. An employer may not retain the Notary's seal after termination of the Notary's employment. Any person who unlawfully possesses a Notary's seal is guilty of a misdemeanor of the second degree (FS 117.05[3][b] and [d]).

Acknowledgment in Lieu of Oath. A notary may not take an acknowledgment in lieu of an oath if an oath is required. (FS 117.03).

Liability and Investigation

Liability for Damages. A Notary and the surety company bonding the Notary may be sued by any person who has been damaged by the Notary's official acts. The surety is liable only up to the amount of the bond, which is $7,500 in Florida, but a Notary may be found liable for any amount of money (FS 117.01[7]).

Employer Liability. If a Notary's official misconduct causes any individual to be financially damaged, then the Notary's employer may be liable to the person for all damages if the Notary was acting within the scope of his or her employment at the time that he or she engaged in the misconduct (FS 117.05[6]).

Complaint and Investigation. A Notary's commission can be suspended or denied for any complaint found to have merit by the Governor. Failure to cooperate or respond to an investigation by the Governor's office regarding such a complaint is also cause for commission suspension or denial. ■

Florida Laws Pertaining to Notaries Public

Reprinted on the following pages are pertinent parts of the Florida Statutes affecting Notaries and notarial acts. For additional reference, history notes are included at the end of each section to show the source of the latest amendment to that section's text.

FLORIDA STATUTES

TITLE X. PUBLIC OFFICERS, EMPLOYEES, AND RECORDS
CHAPTER 117. NOTARIES PUBLIC
PART I. GENERAL PROVISIONS

117.01 Appointment, application, suspension, revocation, application fee, bond, and oath.—

(1) The Governor may appoint as many notaries public as he or she deems necessary, each of whom must be at least 18 years of age and a legal resident of this state. A permanent resident alien may apply and be appointed and shall file with his or her application a recorded Declaration of Domicile. The residence required for appointment must be maintained throughout the term of appointment. A notary public shall be appointed for 4 years and may only use and exercise the office of notary public if he or she is within the boundaries of this state. An applicant must be able to read, write, and understand the English language.

(2) The application for appointment shall be signed and sworn to by the applicant and

shall be accompanied by a fee of $25, together with the $10 commission fee required by s. 113.01, and a surcharge of $4, which $4 is appropriated to the Executive Office of the Governor to be used to educate and assist notaries public. The Executive Office of the Governor may contract with private vendors to provide the services set forth in this section. However, no commission fee shall be required for the issuance of a commission as a notary public to a veteran who served during a period of wartime service, as defined in s. 1.01(14), and who has been rated by the United States Government or the United States Department of Veterans Affairs or its predecessor to have a disability rating of 50 percent or more; such disability is subject to verification by the Secretary of State, who has authority to adopt reasonable procedures to implement this act. The oath of office and notary bond required by this section shall also accompany the application and shall be in a form prescribed by the Department of State which shall require, but not be limited to, the following information: full name, residence address and telephone number, business address and telephone number, date of birth, race, sex, social security number, citizenship status, driver license number or the number of other official state-issued identification, affidavit of good character from someone unrelated to the applicant who has known the applicant for 1 year or more, a list of all professional licenses and commissions issued by the state during the previous 10 years and a statement as to whether or not the applicant has had such license or commission revoked or suspended, and a statement as to whether or not the applicant has been convicted of a felony, and, if there has been a conviction, a statement of the nature of the felony and restoration of civil rights. The applicant may not use a fictitious or assumed name other than a nickname on an application for commission. The application shall be maintained by the Department of State for the full term of a notary commission. A notary public shall notify, in writing, the Department of State of any change in his or her business address, home telephone number, business telephone number, home address, or criminal record within 60 days after such change.

The Governor may require any other information he or she deems necessary for determining whether an applicant is eligible for a notary public commission. Each applicant must swear or affirm on the application that the information on the application is true and correct.

(3) As part of the oath, the applicant must swear that he or she has read this chapter and knows the duties, responsibilities, limitations, and powers of a notary public.

(4) The Governor may suspend a notary public for any of the grounds provided in s. 7, Art. IV of the State Constitution. Grounds constituting malfeasance, misfeasance, or neglect of duty include, but are not limited to, the following:

(a) A material false statement on the application.

(b) A complaint found to have merit by the Governor.

(c) Failure to cooperate or respond to an investigation by the Governor's office or the Department of State regarding a complaint.

(d) Official misconduct as defined in s. 838.022.

(e) False or misleading advertising relating to notary public services.

(f) Unauthorized practice of law.

(g) Failure to report a change in business or home address or telephone number, or failure to submit documentation to request an amended commission after a lawful name change, within the specified period of time.

(h) Commission of fraud, misrepresentation, or any intentional violation of this chapter.

(i) Charging fees in excess of fees authorized by this chapter.

(j) Failure to maintain the bond required by this section.

(5)(a) If a notary public receives notice from the Department of State that his or her office has been declared vacant, the notary shall forthwith mail or deliver to the Secretary of State his or her notary commission.

(b) A notary public who wishes to resign his or her commission, or a notary public who does not maintain legal residence in this state during the entire term of appointment, or a notary public whose resignation is required by the Governor, shall send a signed letter of resignation to the Governor and shall return his or her certificate of notary public commission. The resigning notary public shall destroy his or her official notary public seal of office, unless the Governor requests its return.

(6) No person may be automatically reappointed as a notary public. The application process must be completed regardless of whether an applicant is requesting his or her first notary commission, a renewal of a commission, or any subsequent commission.

(7)(a) A notary public shall, prior to executing the duties of the office and throughout the term of office, give bond, payable to any individual harmed as a result of a breach of duty by the notary public acting in his or her official capacity, in the amount of $7,500, conditioned for the due discharge of the office and shall take an oath that he or she will honestly, diligently, and faithfully discharge the duties of the notary public. The bond shall be approved and filed with the Department of State and executed by a surety company for hire duly authorized to transact business in this state.

(b) Any notary public whose term of appointment extends beyond January 1, 1999, is required to increase the amount of his or her bond to $7,500 only upon reappointment on or after January 1, 1999.

(c) Beginning July 1, 1996, surety companies for hire which process notary public applications, oaths, affidavits of character, and bonds for submission to the Department of State must properly submit these documents in a software and hard copy format approved by the Department of State.

(8) Upon payment to any individual harmed as a result of a breach of duty by the notary public, the entity who has issued the bond for the notary public shall notify the Governor of the payment and the circumstances which led to the claim.

117.021 Electronic notarization.—

(1) Any document requiring notarization may be notarized electronically. The provisions of ss. 117.01, 117.03, 117.04, 117.05(1)-(11), (13), and (14), 117.105, and 117.107 apply to all notarizations under this section.

(2) In performing an electronic notarial act, a notary public shall use an electronic signature that is:

(a) Unique to the notary public;

(b) Capable of independent verification;

(c) Retained under the notary public's sole control and includes access protection through the use of passwords or codes under control of the notary public; and

(d) Attached to or logically associated with the electronic document in a manner that any subsequent alteration to the electronic document displays evidence of the alteration.

(3) When a signature is required to be accompanied by a notary public seal, the requirement is satisfied when the electronic signature of the notary public contains all of the following seal information:

(a) The full name of the notary public exactly as provided on the notary public's application for commission;

(b) The words "Notary Public State of Florida";

(c) The date of expiration of the commission of the notary public; and

(d) The notary public's commission number.

(4) A notary public performing a notarial act with respect to an electronic record shall select the technology to be used for such notarial act. A person may not require the notary public to use a particular technology; however, if the notary public is required by his or her contract or employer to perform notarial acts with respect to electronic records, the contract or employer may require the use of a particular technology for those notarial acts.

(5) Failure of a notary public to comply with any of the requirements of this section may constitute grounds for suspension of the notary public's commission by the Executive Office of the Governor.

(6) The Department of State may adopt rules to ensure the security, reliability, and uniformity of signatures and seals authorized in this section.

(7) The Department of State, in collaboration with the Department of Management Services, shall adopt rules establishing standards for tamper-evident technologies that will indicate any alteration or change to an electronic record after completion of an electronic notarial act. All electronic notarizations performed on or after January 1, 2020, must comply with the adopted standards.

117.03 Administration of oaths. — A notary public may administer an oath and make a certificate thereof when it is necessary for the execution of any writing or document to be published under the seal of a notary public. The notary public may not take an acknowledgment of execution in lieu of an oath if an oath is required.

117.04 Acknowledgments. — A notary public is authorized to take the acknowledgments of deeds and other instruments of writing for record, as fully as other officers of this state.

117.045 Marriages. — A notary public is authorized to solemnize the rites of matrimony. For solemnizing the rites of matrimony, the fee of a notary public may not exceed those provided by law to the clerks of the circuit court for like services.

117.05 Use of notary commission; unlawful use; notary fee; seal; duties; employer liability; name change; advertising; photocopies; penalties.—

(1) A person may not obtain or use a notary public commission in other than his or her legal name, and it is unlawful for a notary public to notarize his or her own signature.

Any person applying for a notary public commission must submit proof of identity to the Department of State. Any person who violates this subsection commits a felony of the third degree, punishable as provided in s. 775.082, s. 775.083, or s. 775.084.

(2)(a) The fee of a notary public may not exceed $10 for any one notarial act, except as provided in s. 117.045 or s. 117.275.

(b) A notary public may not charge a fee for witnessing a vote-by-mail ballot in an election, and must witness such a ballot upon the request of an elector, provided the notarial act is in accordance with the provisions of this chapter.

(3)(a) A notary public seal shall be affixed to all notarized paper documents and shall be of the rubber stamp type and shall include the words "Notary Public-State of Florida."

The seal shall also include the name of the notary public, the date of expiration of the commission of the notary public, and the commission number. The rubber stamp seal must be affixed to the notarized paper document in photographically reproducible black ink. Every notary public shall print, type, or stamp below his or her signature on a paper document his or her name exactly as commissioned. An impression-type seal may be used in addition to the rubber stamp seal, but the rubber stamp seal shall be the official seal for use on a paper document, and the impression-type seal may not be substituted therefor.

(b) The notary public official seal and the certificate of notary public commission are the exclusive property of the notary public and must be kept under the direct and exclusive control of the notary public. The seal and certificate of commission must not be surrendered to an employer upon termination of employment, regardless of whether the employer paid for the seal or for the commission.

(c) A notary public whose official seal is lost, stolen, or believed to be in the possession of another person shall immediately notify the Department of State or the Governor in writing.

(d) Any person who unlawfully possesses a notary public official seal or any papers or copies relating to notarial acts is guilty of a misdemeanor of the second degree, punishable as provided in s. 775.082 or s. 775.083.

(4) When notarizing a signature, a notary public shall complete a jurat or notarial certificate in substantially the same form as those found in subsection (13). The jurat or certificate of acknowledgment shall contain the following elements:

(a) The venue stating the location of the notary public at the time of the notarization in the format, "State of Florida, County of."

(b) The type of notarial act performed, an oath or an acknowledgment, evidenced by the words "sworn" or "acknowledged."

(c) Whether the signer personally appeared before the notary public at the time of the notarization by physical presence or by means of audio-video communication technology as authorized under part II of this chapter.

(d) The exact date of the notarial act.

(e) The name of the person whose signature is being notarized. It is presumed, absent such specific notation by the notary public, that notarization is to all signatures.

(f) The specific type of identification the notary public is relying upon in identifying the signer, either based on personal knowledge or satisfactory evidence specified in subsection (5).

(g) The notary public's official signature.

(h) The notary public's name, which must be typed, printed, or stamped below the signature.

(i) The notary public's official seal affixed below or to either side of the notary public's signature.

(5) A notary public may not notarize a signature on a document unless he or she personally knows, or has satisfactory evidence, that the person whose signature is to be notarized is the individual who is described in and who is executing the instrument. A

notary public shall certify in the certificate of acknowledgment or jurat the type of identification, either based on personal knowledge or other form of identification, upon which the notary public is relying. In the case of an online notarization, the online notary public shall comply with the requirements set forth in part II of this chapter.

(a) For purposes of this subsection, the term "personally knows" means having an acquaintance, derived from association with the individual, which establishes the individual's identity with at least a reasonable certainty.

(b) For the purposes of this subsection, the term "satisfactory evidence" means the absence of any information, evidence, or other circumstances which would lead a reasonable person to believe that the person whose signature is to be notarized is not the person he or she claims to be and any one of the following:

1. The sworn written statement of one credible witness personally known to the notary public or the sworn written statement of two credible witnesses whose identities are proven to the notary public upon the presentation of satisfactory evidence that each of the following is true:

a. That the person whose signature is to be notarized is the person named in the document;

b. That the person whose signature is to be notarized is personally known to the witnesses;

c. That it is the reasonable belief of the witnesses that the circumstances of the person whose signature is to be notarized are such that it would be very difficult or impossible for that person to obtain another acceptable form of identification;

d. That it is the reasonable belief of the witnesses that the person whose signature is to be notarized does not possess any of the identification documents specified in subparagraph 2.; and

e. That the witnesses do not have a financial interest in nor are parties to the underlying transaction; or

2. Reasonable reliance on the presentation to the notary public of any one of the following forms of identification, if the document is current or has been issued within the past 5 years and bears a serial or other identifying number:

a. A Florida identification card or driver license issued by the public agency authorized to issue driver licenses;

b. A passport issued by the Department of State of the United States;

c. A passport issued by a foreign government if the document is stamped by the United States Bureau of Citizenship and Immigration Services;

d. A driver license or an identification card issued by a public agency authorized to issue driver licenses in a state other than Florida or in a territory of the United States, or Canada or Mexico;

e. An identification card issued by any branch of the armed forces of the United States;

f. A veteran health identification card issued by the United States Department of Veterans Affairs;

g. An inmate identification card issued on or after January 1, 1991, by the Florida Department of Corrections for an inmate who is in the custody of the department;

h. An inmate identification card issued by the United States Department of Justice, Bureau of Prisons, for an inmate who is in the custody of the department;

i. A sworn, written statement from a sworn law enforcement officer that the forms of identification for an inmate in an institution of confinement were confiscated upon confinement and that the person named in the document is the person whose signature is to be notarized; or

j. An identification card issued by the United States Bureau of Citizenship and Immigration Services.

(6) The employer of a notary public shall be liable to the persons involved for all damages proximately caused by the notary's official misconduct, if the notary public was acting within the scope of his or her employment at the time the notary engaged in the official misconduct.

(7) Any person who acts as or otherwise willfully impersonates a notary public while not lawfully appointed and commissioned to perform notarial acts is guilty of a misdemeanor of the second degree, punishable as provided in s. 775.082 or s. 775.083.

(8) Any notary public who knowingly acts as a notary public after his or her commission has expired is guilty of a misdemeanor of the second degree, punishable as provided in s. 775.082 or s. 775.083.

(9) Any notary public who lawfully changes his or her name shall, within 60 days after such change, request an amended commission from the Secretary of State and shall send $25, his or her current commission, and a notice of change form, obtained from the Secretary of State, which shall include the new name and contain a specimen of his or her official signature. The Secretary of State shall issue an amended commission to the notary public in the new name. A rider to the notary public's bond must accompany the notice of change form. After submitting the required notice of change form and rider to the Secretary of State, the notary public may continue to perform notarial acts in his or her former name for 60 days or until receipt of the amended commission, whichever date is earlier.

(10) A notary public who is not an attorney who advertises the services of a notary public in a language other than English, whether by radio, television, signs, pamphlets, newspapers, or other written communication, with the exception of a single desk plaque, shall post or otherwise include with the advertisement a notice in English and in the language used for the advertisement. The notice shall be of a conspicuous size, if in writing, and shall state: "I AM NOT AN ATTORNEY LICENSED TO PRACTICE LAW IN THE STATE OF FLORIDA, AND I MAY NOT GIVE LEGAL ADVICE OR ACCEPT FEES FOR LEGAL ADVICE." If the advertisement is by radio or television, the statement may be modified but must include substantially the same message.

(11) Literal translation of the phrase "Notary Public" into a language other than English is prohibited in an advertisement for notarial services.

(12)(a) A notary public may supervise the making of a copy of a tangible or an electronic record or the printing of an electronic record and attest to the trueness of the copy or of the printout, provided the document is neither a vital record in this state, another state, a territory of the United States, or another country, nor a public record, if a copy can be made by the custodian of the public record.

(b) A notary public must use a certificate in substantially the following form in notarizing an attested copy:

> STATE OF FLORIDA
> COUNTY OF
>
> On this day of_____ (year) I attest that the preceding or attached document is a true, exact, complete, and unaltered photocopy made by me of _____

(description of document) presented to me by the document's custodian, and, to the best of my knowledge, that the photocopied document is neither a vital record nor a public record, certified copies of which are available from an official source other than a notary public.

(Official Notary Signature and Notary Seal)
(Name of Notary Typed, Printed or Stamped)

(c) A notary public must use a certificate in substantially the following form in notarizing a copy of a tangible or an electronic record or a printout of an electronic record:

STATE OF FLORIDA
COUNTY OF

On this day of _____ (year) I attest that the preceding or attached document is a true, exact, complete, and unaltered (copy of a tangible or an electronic record presented to me by the document's custodian) or a (printout made by me from such record). If a printout, I further attest that, at the time of printing, no security features, if any, present on the electronic record, indicated that the record had been altered since execution.

(Signature of Notary Public - State of Florida)
(Print, Type, or Stamp Commissioned Name of Notary Public)

(13) The following notarial certificates are sufficient for the purposes indicated, if completed with the information required by this chapter. The specification of forms under this subsection does not preclude the use of other forms.

(a) For an oath or affirmation:

STATE OF FLORIDA
COUNTY OF

Sworn to (or affirmed) and subscribed before me by means of ☐ physical presence or ☐ online notarization, this day of _____ (year) by _____ (name of person making statement).

(Signature of Notary Public - State of Florida)
(Print, Type, or Stamp Commissioned Name of Notary Public)
Personally Known _____ OR Produced Identification _____
Type of Identification Produced _____

(b) For an acknowledgment in an individual capacity:

STATE OF FLORIDA
COUNTY OF

The foregoing instrument was acknowledged before me by means of ☐ physical presence or ☐ online notarization, this day of _____ (year) by _____ (name of person acknowledging).

(Signature of Notary Public - State of Florida)
(Print, Type, or Stamp Commissioned Name of Notary Public)

Personally Known _____ OR Produced Identification _____
Type of Identification Produced _____

(c) For an acknowledgment in a representative capacity:

> STATE OF FLORIDA
> COUNTY OF
>
> The foregoing instrument was acknowledged before me by means of ☐ physical presence or ☐ online notarization, this _____ day of _____ (year) by _____ (name of person) as _____ (type of authority, e.g. officer, trustee, attorney in fact) for _____ (name of party on behalf of whom instrument was executed)
>
> (Signature of Notary Public - State of Florida)
> (Print, Type, or Stamp Commissioned Name of Notary Public)
> Personally Known _____ OR Produced Identification _____
> Type of Identification Produced _____

(14) A notary public must make reasonable accommodations to provide notarial services to persons with disabilities.

(a) A notary public may notarize the signature of a person who is blind after the notary public has read the entire instrument to that person.

(b) A notary public may notarize the signature of a person who signs with a mark if:

1. The document signing is witnessed by two disinterested persons;

2. The notary public prints the person's first name at the beginning of the designated signature line and the person's last name at the end of the designated signature line; and

3. The notary public prints the words "his (or her) mark" below the person's signature mark.

(c) The following notarial certificates are sufficient for the purpose of notarizing for a person who signs with a mark:

1. For an oath or affirmation:

> (First Name) (Last Name)
> His (or Her) Mark
>
> STATE OF FLORIDA
> COUNTY OF
>
> Sworn to and subscribed before me by means of ☐ physical presence or ☐ online notarization, this day of _____ (year) by _____ (name of person making statement) who signed with a mark in the presence of these witnesses: _____
> _____
>
> (Signature of Notary Public - State of Florida)
> (Print, Type, or Stamp Commissioned Name of Notary Public)
> Personally Known _____ OR Produced Identification _____
> Type of Identification Produced _____

2. For an acknowledgment in an individual capacity:

(First Name) (Last Name)
His (or Her) Mark

STATE OF FLORIDA
COUNTY OF

The foregoing instrument was acknowledged before me by means of ☐ physical presence or ☐ online notarization, this _____ day of _____ (year) by _____ (name of person acknowledging) who signed with a mark in the presence of these witnesses: _____

(Signature of Notary Public - State of Florida)
(Print, Type, or Stamp Commissioned Name of Notary Public)
Personally Known _____ OR Produced Identification _____
Type of Identification Produced _____
Type of Identification Produced _____

(d) A notary public may sign the name of a person whose signature is to be notarized when that person is physically unable to sign or make a signature mark on a document if:

1. The person with a disability directs the notary public to sign in his or her presence by verbal, written, or other means;

2. The document signing is witnessed by two disinterested persons; and

3. The notary public writes below the signature the following statement: "Signature affixed by notary, pursuant to s. 117.05(14), Florida Statutes," and states the circumstances and the means by which the notary public was directed to sign the notarial certificate.

The notary public must maintain the proof of direction and authorization to sign on behalf of the person with a disability for 10 years from the date of the notarial act.

(e) The following notarial certificates are sufficient for the purpose of notarizing for a person with a disability who directs the notary public to sign his or her name:

1. For an oath or affirmation:

STATE OF FLORIDA
COUNTY OF

Sworn to (or affirmed) before me by means of ☐ physical presence or ☐ online notarization, this _____ day of _____ (year) by _____ (name of person making statement) and subscribed by _____ (name of notary) at the direction of _____ (name of person making statement) by _____ (written, verbal, or other means) and in the presence of these witnesses: _____

(Signature of Notary Public - State of Florida)
(Print, Type, or Stamp Commissioned Name of Notary Public)
Personally Known _____ OR Produced Identification _____
Type of Identification Produced _____

2. For an acknowledgment in an individual capacity:

STATE OF FLORIDA
COUNTY OF

The foregoing instrument was acknowledged before me by means of ☐ physical presence or ☐ online notarization, this _____ day of _____, _____ (year), by _____(name of person acknowledging) and subscribed by _____ (name of notary) at the direction of _____ (name of person acknowledging), and in the presence of these witnesses: _____

(Signature of Notary Public - State of Florida)
(Print, Type, or Stamp Commissioned Name of Notary Public)
Personally Known _____ OR Produced Identification _____
Type of Identification Produced _____

117.06 Validity of acts prior to April 1, 1903. — Any and all notarial acts that were done by any notary public in the state prior to April 1, 1903, which would have been valid had not the term of office of the notary public expired, are declared to be valid.

117.10 Law enforcement and correctional officers; administration of oaths.—

(1) For purposes of this section, the term "reliable electronic means" means the signing and transmission of a document through means compliant with criminal justice information system security measures. Such signing and transmission must be made by an affiant to an officer authorized to administer oaths under subsection (2) under circumstances that indicate that the document was submitted by the affiant.

(2) Law enforcement officers, correctional officers, and correctional probation officers, as defined in s. 943.10, and traffic accident investigation officers and traffic infraction enforcement officers, as described in s. 316.640, are authorized to administer oaths by reliable electronic means or in the physical presence of an affiant when engaged in the performance of official duties. Sections 117.01, 117.04, 117.045, 117.05, and 117.103 do not apply to this section. An officer may not notarize his or her own signature.

(3) An oath administered pursuant to this section is an acceptable method of verification as provided under s. 92.525.

117.103 Certification of notary's authority by Secretary of State. — A notary public is not required to record his or her notary public commission in an office of a clerk of the circuit court. If certification of the notary public's commission is required, it must be obtained from the Secretary of State. Upon the receipt of a written request and a fee of $10 payable to the Secretary of State, the Secretary of State shall issue a certificate of notarial authority, in a form prescribed by the Secretary of State, which shall include a statement explaining the legal qualifications and authority of a notary public in this state.

117.105 False or fraudulent acknowledgments; penalty. — A notary public who falsely or fraudulently takes an acknowledgment of an instrument as a notary public or who falsely or fraudulently makes a certificate as a notary public or who falsely takes or receives an acknowledgment of the signature on a written instrument is guilty of a felony of the third degree, punishable as provided in s. 775.082, s. 775.083, or s. 775.084.

117.107 Prohibited acts.—

(1) A notary public may not use a name or initial in signing certificates other than that by which the notary public is commissioned.

(2) A notary public may not sign notarial certificates using a facsimile signature stamp unless the notary public has a physical disability that limits or prohibits his or her

ability to make a written signature and unless the notary public has first submitted written notice to the Department of State with an exemplar of the facsimile signature stamp. This subsection does not apply to or prohibit the use of an electronic signature and seal by a notary public who is registered as an online notary public to perform an electronic or online notarization in accordance with this chapter.

(3) A notary public may not affix his or her signature to a blank form of affidavit or certificate of acknowledgment and deliver that form to another person with the intent that it be used as an affidavit or acknowledgment.

(4) A notary public may not take the acknowledgment of or administer an oath to a person whom the notary public actually knows to have been adjudicated mentally incapacitated by a court of competent jurisdiction, where the acknowledgment or oath necessitates the exercise of a right that has been removed pursuant to s. 744.3215(2) or

(3), and where the person has not been restored to capacity as a matter of record.

(5) A notary public may not notarize a signature on a document if it appears that the person is mentally incapable of understanding the nature and effect of the document at the time of notarization.

(6) A notary public may not take the acknowledgment of a person who does not speak or understand the English language, unless the nature and effect of the instrument to be notarized is translated into a language which the person does understand.

(7) A notary public may not change anything in a written instrument after it has been signed by anyone.

(8) A notary public may not amend a notarial certificate after the notarization is complete.

(9) A notary public may not notarize a signature on a document if the person whose signature is being notarized does not appear before the notary public either by means of physical presence or by means of audio-video communication technology as authorized under part II of this chapter at the time the signature is notarized. Any notary public who violates this subsection is guilty of a civil infraction, punishable by penalty not exceeding $5,000, and such violation constitutes malfeasance and misfeasance in the conduct of official duties. It is no defense to the civil infraction specified in this subsection that the notary public acted without intent to defraud. A notary public who violates this subsection with the intent to defraud is guilty of violating s. 117.105.

(10) A notary public may not notarize a signature on a document if the document is incomplete or blank. However, an endorsement or assignment in blank of a negotiable or nonnegotiable note and the assignment in blank of any instrument given as security for such note is not deemed incomplete.

(11) A notary public may not notarize a signature on a document if the person whose signature is to be notarized is the spouse, son, daughter, mother, or father of the notary public.

(12) A notary public may not notarize a signature on a document if the notary public has a financial interest in or is a party to the underlying transaction; however, a notary public who is an employee may notarize a signature for his or her employer, and this employment does not constitute a financial interest in the transaction nor make the notary a party to the transaction under this subsection as long as he or she does not receive a benefit other than his or her salary and the fee for services as a notary public authorized by law. For purposes of this subsection, a notary public who is an attorney does not have a financial interest in and is not a party to the underlying transaction evidenced by a notarized document if he or she notarizes a signature on

that document for a client for whom he or she serves as an attorney of record and he or she has no interest in the document other than the fee paid to him or her for legal services and the fee authorized by law for services as a notary public.

117.108 Validity of acts, seals, and certificates prior to January 1, 1995. — A notarial act performed, a notarial certificate signed, or a notarial seal used by any notary public before January 1, 1995, which would have been valid under the laws in effect in this state on January 1, 1991, is valid.

PART II. ONLINE NOTARIZATIONS

117.201 Definitions. — As used in this part, the term:

(1) "Appear before," "before," or "in the presence of" means:

(a) In the physical presence of another person; or

(b) Outside of the physical presence of another person, but able to see, hear, and communicate with the person by means of audio-video communication technology.

(2) Audio-video communication technology" means technology in compliance with applicable law which enables real-time, two-way communication using electronic means in which participants are able to see, hear, and communicate with one another.

(3) "Credential analysis" means a process or service, in compliance with applicable law, in which a third party aids a notary public in affirming the validity of a government-issued identification credential and data thereon through review of public or proprietary data sources.

(4) "Electronic," "electronic record," or "electronic signature" has the same meaning as provided in s. 668.50.

(5) "Errors and omissions insurance" means a type of insurance that provides coverage for potential errors or omissions in or relating to the notarial act and is maintained, as applicable, by the online notary public or his or her employer, or a Remote Online Notarization service provider.

(6) "Government-issued identification credential" means any approved credential for verifying identity under s. 117.05(5)(b)2. However, for an online notarization of a principal not located within the United States, a passport issued by a foreign government not including the stamp of the United States Bureau of Citizenship and Immigration Services may be used as a government-issued identification credential to verify the principal's identity.

(7) "Identity proofing" means a process or service in compliance with applicable law in which a third party affirms the identity of an individual through use of public or proprietary data sources, which may include by means of knowledge-based authentication or biometric verification.

(8) "Knowledge-based authentication" means a form of identity proofing based on a set of questions which pertain to an individual and are formulated from public or proprietary data sources.

(9) "Online notarization" means the performance of a notarial act using electronic means in which the principal or any witness appears before the notary public by means of audio-video communication technology.

(10) "Online notary public" means a notary public commissioned under part I of this chapter, a civil-law notary appointed under chapter 118, or a commissioner of deeds

appointed under part IV of chapter 721, who has registered with the Department of State to perform online notarizations under this part.

(11) "Physical presence" means being in the same physical location as another person and close enough to see, hear, communicate with, and exchange credentials with that person.

(12) "Principal" means an individual whose electronic signature is acknowledged, witnessed, or attested to in an online notarization or who takes an oath or affirmation administered by the online notary public.

(13) "Record" means information that is inscribed on a tangible medium or that is stored in an electronic or other medium and is retrievable in perceivable form, including public records as defined in s. 119.011.

(14) "Remote Online Notarization service provider" or "RON service provider" means a person that provides audio-video communication technology and related processes, services, software, data storage, or other services to online notaries public for the purpose of directly facilitating their performance of online notarizations, in compliance with the requirements of this chapter and any rules adopted by the Department of State pursuant to s. 117.295.

(15) "Remote presentation" means transmission of an image of a government-issued identification credential that is of sufficient quality to enable the online notary public to identify the individual seeking the notary's services and to perform credential analysis through audio-video communication technology.

117.209 Authority to perform online notarizations.—

(1) An online notary public may perform any of the functions authorized under part I of this chapter as an online notarization by complying with the requirements of this part and any rules adopted by the Department of State pursuant to s. 117.295, excluding solemnizing the rites of matrimony.

(2) If a notarial act requires a principal to appear before or in the presence of the online notary public, the principal may appear before the online notary public by means of audio-video communication technology that meets the requirements of this part and any rules adopted by the Department of State pursuant to s. 117.295.

(3) An online notary public physically located in this state may perform an online notarization as authorized under this part, regardless of whether the principal or any witnesses are physically located in this state at the time of the online notarization. A commissioner of deeds registered as an online notary public may perform an online notarization while physically located within or outside the state in accordance with the territorial limits of its jurisdiction and other limitations and requirements otherwise applicable to notarial acts by commissioners of deeds.

(4) The validity of an online notarization performed by an online notary public registered in this state shall be determined by applicable laws of this state regardless of the physical location of the principal or any witnesses at the time of the notarial act.

117.215 Relation to other laws.—

(1) If a provision of law requires a notary public or other authorized official of this state to notarize a signature or a statement, to take an acknowledgment of an instrument, or to administer an oath or affirmation so that a document may be sworn, affirmed, made under oath, or subject to penalty of perjury, an online notarization performed in accordance with the provisions of this part and any rules adopted hereunder satisfies such requirement.

(2) If a provision of law requires a signature or an act to be witnessed, compliance with the online electronic witnessing standards prescribed in s. 117.285 and any rules adopted thereunder satisfies that requirement.

117.225 Registration; qualifications. — A notary public, a civil-law notary appointed under chapter 118, or a commissioner of deeds appointed under part IV of chapter 721 may complete registration as an online notary public with the Department of State by:

(1) Holding a current commission as a notary public under part I of this chapter, an appointment as a civil-law notary under chapter 118, or an appointment as a commissioner of deeds under part IV of chapter 721, and submitting his or her commission or appointment number.

(2) Certifying that the notary public, civil-law notary, or commissioner of deeds registering as an online notary public has completed a classroom or online course covering the duties, obligations, and technology requirements for serving as an online notary public.

(3) Paying a notary public registration fee as required by s. 113.01.

(4) Submitting a registration as an online notary public to the Department of State, signed and sworn to by the registrant.

(5) Identifying the RON service provider or providers whose audio-video communication technology and processes for credential analysis and identity-proofing technologies the registrant intends to use for online notarizations.

(6) Providing evidence satisfactory to the Department of State that the registrant has obtained a bond in the amount of $25,000, payable to any individual harmed as a result of a breach of duty by the registrant acting in his or her official capacity as an online notary public, conditioned for the due discharge of the office, and on such terms as are specified in rule by the Department of State as reasonably necessary to protect the public. The bond shall be approved and filed with the Department of State and executed by a surety company duly authorized to transact business in this state. Compliance by an online notary public with this requirement shall satisfy the requirement of obtaining a bond under s. 117.01(7).

(7) Providing evidence satisfactory to the Department of State that the registrant acting in his or her capacity as an online notary public is covered by an errors and omissions insurance policy from an insurer authorized to transact business in this state, in the minimum amount of $25,000 and on such terms as are specified by rule by the Department of State as reasonably necessary to protect the public.

117.231 Remote administration of certain oaths.—

(1) When taking the oath of an individual who is testifying at any court proceeding, deposition, arbitration, or public hearing and who is outside of the physical presence of the notary public, the notary public may fulfill the requirements of s. 117.05 using audiovideo communication technology.

(2) When taking an oath of admission to The Florida Bar from an individual who is outside of the physical presence of the notary public, the notary public may fulfill the requirements of s. 117.05 using audio-video communication technology.

(3) If an individual is located outside of this state at the time the notary public is to take the individual's oath under this section, consent from the individual must be obtained to take his or her oath using audio-video communication technology pursuant to this section.

(4) When taking an oath under this section, the notary public is not required to be an online notary public or to use a RON service provider.

117.235 Performance of notarial acts.—

(1) An online notary public is subject to part I of this chapter to the same extent as a notary public appointed and commissioned only under that part, including the provisions of s. 117.021 relating to electronic notarizations.

(2) An online notary public may perform notarial acts as provided by part I of this chapter in addition to performing online notarizations as authorized and pursuant to the provisions of this part.

117.245 Electronic journal of online notarizations.—

(1) An online notary public shall keep one or more secure electronic journals of online notarizations performed by the online notary public. For each online notarization, the electronic journal entry must contain all of the following:

(a) The date and time of the notarization.

(b) The type of notarial act performed, whether an oath or acknowledgment.

(c) The type, the title, or a description of the electronic record or proceeding.

(d) The name and address of each principal involved in the transaction or proceeding.

(e) Evidence of identity of each principal involved in the transaction or proceeding in either of the following forms:

1. A statement that the person is personally known to the online notary public; or

2.a. A notation of the type of government-issued identification credential provided to the online notary public;

b. An indication that the government-issued identification credential satisfied the credential analysis; and

c. An indication that the principal satisfactorily passed the identity proofing.

(f) The fee, if any, charged for the notarization.

(2) The RON service provider shall retain an uninterrupted and unedited copy of the recording of the audio-video communication in which an online notarization is performed. The online notary public shall ensure that the recording includes all of the following:

(a) Appearance by the principal and any witness before the online notary public.

(b) Confirmation of the identity of the principal and any witness.

(c) A general description or identification of the records to be signed.

(d) At the commencement of the recording, recitation by the online notary public of information sufficient to identify the notarial act.

(e) A declaration by the principal that his or her signature on the record is knowingly and voluntarily made.

(f) All of the actions and spoken words of the principal, notary public, and any required witness during the entire online notarization, including the signing of any records before the online notary public.

(3) The online notary public shall take reasonable steps to:

(a) Ensure the integrity, security, and authenticity of online notarizations.

(b) Maintain a backup record of the electronic journal required by subsection (1).

(c) Protect the electronic journal, the backup record, and any other records received by the online notary public from unauthorized access or use.

(4) The electronic journal required under subsection (1) and the recordings of audio-video communications required under subsection (2) shall be maintained for at least 10 years after the date of the notarial act. However, a full copy of the recording of the audiovideo communication required under subsection (2) relating to an online notarization session that involves the signing of an electronic will must be maintained by a qualified custodian in accordance with chapters 731 and 732. The Department of State maintains jurisdiction over the electronic journal and audio-video communication recordings to investigate notarial misconduct for a period of 10 years after the date of the notarial act.

The online notary public, a guardian of an incapacitated online notary public, or the personal representative of a deceased online notary public may, by contract with a secure repository in accordance with any rules established under this chapter, delegate to the repository the online notary public's duty to retain the electronic journal, provided that the Department of State is notified of such delegation of retention duties to the repository within 30 days thereafter, including the effective date of the delegation and the address and contact information for the repository. If an online notary public delegates to a secure repository under this section, the online notary public shall make an entry in his or her electronic journal identifying such repository and provide notice to the Department of State as required in this subsection. A RON service provider may, by contract with a secure repository in accordance with any rules established under this chapter, delegate to the repository the RON service provider's duty to retain the required recordings of audiovideo communications, provided that the Department of State is notified of such delegation of retention duties to the repository within 30 days thereafter, including the effective date of the delegation and the address and contact information for the repository. During any delegation under this subsection, the secure repository shall fulfill the responsibilities of the online notary public or RON service provider to provide copies or access under s. 117.255(2) and (3).

(5) An omitted or incomplete entry in the electronic journal does not impair the validity of the notarial act or of the electronic record which was notarized, but may be introduced as evidence to establish violations of this chapter; as evidence of possible fraud, forgery, impersonation, duress, incapacity, undue influence, minority, illegality, or unconscionability; or for other evidentiary purposes. However, if the recording of the audio-video communication required under subsection (2) relating to the online notarization of the execution of an electronic will cannot be produced by the RON service provider, the online notary public, or the qualified custodian, the electronic will shall be treated as a lost or destroyed will subject to s. 733.207.

117.255 Use of electronic journal, signature, and seal.—

(1) An online notary public shall:

(a) Take reasonable steps to ensure that any registered device used to create an electronic seal is current and has not been revoked or terminated by the issuing or registering authority of the device.

(b) Keep the electronic journal and electronic seal secure and under his or her sole control, which includes access protection using passwords or codes under control of the online notary public. The online notary public may not allow another person to use the online notary public's electronic journal, electronic signature, or electronic seal, other than a RON service provider or other authorized person providing services to an online notary public to facilitate performance of online notarizations.

(c) Attach or logically associate the electronic signature and seal to the electronic notarial certificate of an electronic record in a manner that is capable of independent verification using tamper-evident technology that renders any subsequent change or modification to the electronic record evident.

(d) Notify an appropriate law enforcement agency and the Department of State of any unauthorized use of or compromise to the security of the electronic journal, official electronic signature, or electronic seal within 7 days after discovery of such unauthorized use or compromise to security.

(2) An online notary public shall provide electronic copies of pertinent entries in the electronic journal, and a RON service provider shall provide access to the related audiovideo communication recordings, or a copy thereof, to the following persons upon request:

(a) The parties to an electronic record notarized by the online notary public;

(b) The qualified custodian of an electronic will notarized by the online notary public;

(c) The title agent, settlement agent, or title insurer who insured the electronic record or engaged the online notary public with regard to a real estate transaction;

(d) Any person who is asked to accept a power of attorney that was notarized by the online notary public;

(e) The Department of State pursuant to a notary misconduct investigation;

(f) Any other persons pursuant to a subpoena, court order, law enforcement investigation, or other lawful inspection demand;

(g) With respect to audio-video communication recordings of an online notarization, the online notary public performing that notarization; and

(h) With respect to electronic copies of pertinent entries in the electronic journal, the RON service provider used for the online notarizations associated with those entries.

(3) The online notary public may charge a fee not to exceed $20 per transaction record for making and delivering electronic copies of a given series of related electronic records, and a RON service provider may charge a fee not to exceed $20 for providing access to, or a copy of, the related audio-video communication records, except such copies or access must be provided without charge if requested by any of the following within the 10-year period specified in s. 117.245(4):

(a) A party to the electronic record;

(b) In a real estate transaction, the title agent, settlement agent, or title insurer who insured the electronic record or engaged the online notary public with regard to such transaction;

(c) The Department of State pursuant to an investigation relating to the official misconduct of an online notary public;

(d) The qualified custodian of an electronic will notarized by the online notary public;

(e) With respect to audio-video communication recordings of an online notarization, the online notary public performing that notarization; or

(f) With respect to electronic copies of a given series of related electronic records, the RON service provider used for the online notarization of those records.

If the online notary public or RON service provider charges a fee, the online notary public or RON service provider must disclose the amount of such fee to the requester before making the electronic copies or providing access to, or making a copy of, the requested audio-video communication recordings.

117.265 Online notarization procedures.—

(1) An online notary public physically located in this state may perform an online notarization that meets the requirements of this part regardless of whether the principal or any witnesses are physically located in this state at the time of the online notarization. A commissioner of deeds registered as an online notary public may perform an online notarization while physically located within or outside of this state in accordance with the territorial limits of its jurisdiction and other limitations and requirements otherwise applicable to notarial acts by commissioners of deeds. An online notarization performed in accordance with this chapter is deemed to have been performed within this state and is governed by the applicable laws of this state.

(2) In performing an online notarization, an online notary public shall confirm the identity of a principal and any witness appearing online, at the time that the signature is taken, by using audio-video communication technology and processes that meet the requirements of this part and of any rules adopted hereunder and record the two-way audio-video conference session between the notary public and the principal and any witnesses. A principal may not act in the capacity of a witness for his or her own signature in an online notarization.

(3) In performing an online notarization of a principal not located within this state, an online notary public must confirm, either verbally or through the principal's written consent, that the principal desires for the notarial act to be performed by a Florida notary public and under the general law of this state.

(4) An online notary public shall confirm the identity of the principal by:

(a) Personal knowledge of each principal; or

(b) All of the following, as such criteria may be modified or supplemented in rules adopted by the Department of State pursuant to s. 117.295:

1. Remote presentation of a government-issued identification credential by each principal.

2. Credential analysis of each government-issued identification credential.

3. Identity proofing of each principal in the form of knowledge-based authentication or another method of identity proofing that conforms to the standards of this chapter.

If the online notary public is unable to satisfy subparagraphs 1.-3., or if the databases consulted for identity proofing do not contain sufficient information to permit authentication, the online notary public may not perform the online notarization.

(5)(a) An online notary public shall select the RON service provider to be used to perform an online notarization, and a person may not require the online notary public to use a particular RON service provider; however, if the online notary public is required by his or her contract or employer to perform online notarizations, the contract or employer may require the use of a particular RON service provider for those online notarizations.

(b) An online notary public may change his or her RON service provider or providers from time to time, but shall notify the Department of State of such change, and its effective date, within 30 days thereafter.

(6) The online notary public or his or her RON service provider shall take reasonable steps to ensure that the audio-video communication technology used in an online notarization is secure from unauthorized interception.

(7) The electronic notarial certificate for an online notarization must include a notation that the notarization is an online notarization which may be satisfied by placing the term "online notary" in or adjacent to the online notary public's seal.

(8) Except where otherwise expressly provided in this part, the provisions of part I of this chapter apply to an online notarization and an online notary public.

(9) Any failure to comply with the online notarization procedures set forth in this section does not impair the validity of the notarial act or the electronic record that was notarized, but may be introduced as evidence to establish violations of this chapter or as an indication of possible fraud, forgery, impersonation, duress, incapacity, undue influence, minority, illegality, or unconscionability, or for other evidentiary purposes.

This subsection may not be construed to alter the duty of an online notary public to comply with this chapter and any rules adopted hereunder.

117.275 Fees for online notarization. — An online notary public or the employer of such online notary public may charge a fee, not to exceed $25, for performing an online notarial act under this part. Fees for services other than notarial acts, including the services of a RON service provider, are not governed by this section. A RON service provider's services are also not considered closing services, as defined in s. 627.7711, and a fee for those services may be separately charged.

117.285 Supervising the witnessing of electronic records. — Supervising the witnessing of an electronic record by an online notary public in accordance with this section is a notarial act. An online notary public may supervise the witnessing of electronic records by complying with the online notarization procedures of this part and using the same audio-video communication technology used for online notarization by a principal, as follows:

(1) The witness may be in the physical presence of the principal or remote from the principal provided the witness and principal are using audio-video communication technology.

(2) If the witness is remote from the principal and viewing and communicating with the principal by means of audio-video communication technology, the principal's and witness's identities must be verified in accordance with the procedures for identifying a principal as set forth in s. 117.265(4). If the witness is in the physical presence of the principal, the witness must confirm his or her identity by stating his or her name and current address on the audio-video recording as part of the act of witnessing.

(3) The act of witnessing an electronic signature means the witness is either in the physical presence of the principal or present through audio-video communication technology at the time the principal affixes the electronic signature and the witness hears the principal make a statement to the effect that the principal has signed the electronic record.

(4) A witness remote from the principal and appearing through audio-video communication technology must verbally confirm that he or she is a resident of and physically located within the United States or a territory of the United States at the time of witnessing.

(5) Notwithstanding subsections (2) and (3), if an electronic record to be signed is a

will under chapter 732; a revocable trust with testamentary aspects as described in s. 736.0403(2)(b); a health care advance directive; an agreement concerning succession or a waiver of spousal rights under s. 732.701 or s. 732.702, respectively; or a power of attorney authorizing any of the transactions enumerated in s. 709.2208, all of the following apply when fewer than two witnesses are in the physical presence of the principal:

(a) Prior to facilitating witnessing of an instrument by means of audio-video communication technology, a RON service provider shall require the principal to answer the following questions in substantially the following form:

1. Are you under the influence of any drug or alcohol today that impairs your ability to make decisions?

2. Do you have any physical or mental condition or long-term disability that impairs your ability to perform the normal activities of daily living?

3. Do you require assistance with daily care?

(b) If any question required under paragraph (a) is answered in the affirmative, the principal's signature on the instrument may only be validly witnessed by witnesses in the physical presence of the principal at the time of signing.

(c) Subsequent to submission of the answers required under paragraph (a), the RON service provider shall give the principal written notice in substantially the following form:

NOTICE: If you are a vulnerable adult as defined in s. 415.102, Florida Statutes, the documents you are about to sign are not valid if witnessed by means of audio-video communication technology. If you suspect you may be a vulnerable adult, you should have witnesses physically present with you before signing.

(d) The act of witnessing an electronic signature through the witness's presence by audio-video communication technology is valid only if, during the audio-video communication, the principal provides verbal answers to all of the following questions, each of which must be asked by the online notary public in substantially the following form:

1. Are you currently married? If so, name your spouse.

2. Please state the names of anyone who assisted you in accessing this video conference today.

3. Please state the names of anyone who assisted you in preparing the documents you are signing today.

4. Where are you currently located?

5. Who is in the room with you?

(e) An online notary public shall consider the responses to the questions specified in paragraph (d) in carrying out of the duties of a notary public as set forth in s. 117.107(5).

(f) A principal's responses to the questions in paragraphs (a) and (d) may be offered as evidence regarding the validity of the instrument, but an incorrect answer may not serve as the sole basis to invalidate an instrument.

(g) The presence of a witness with the principal at the time of signing by means of audio-video communication technology is not effective for witnessing the signature of a principal who is a vulnerable adult as defined in s. 415.102. The contestant of an electronic record has the burden of proving that the principal was a vulnerable adult at the time of executing the electronic record.

(h) Nothing in this subsection shall:

1. Preclude a power of attorney, which includes banking or investment powers enumerated in s. 709.2208, from being effective with respect to any other authority granted therein or with respect to the agent's authority in connection with a real property, commercial, or consumer transaction or loan, to exercise any power specified therein or to execute and deliver instruments obligating the principal or to draw upon the proceeds of such transaction or loan; or

2. Affect the nontestamentary aspects of a revocable trust under chapter 736.

(i) The electronic record containing an instrument signed by witnesses who were present with the principal by means of audio-video communication technology shall contain a perceptible indication of their presence by such means.

(j) This subsection does not affect the application of s. 709.2119.

(k) The requirements of this subsection do not apply if there are at least two witnesses in the physical presence of the principal at the time of the notarial act.

(6) Pursuant to subpoena, court order, an authorized law enforcement inquiry, or other lawful request, a RON service provider or online notary public shall provide:

(a) The last known address of each witness who witnessed the signing of an electronic record using audio-video communication technology under this section.

(b) A principal's responses to the questions in paragraph (5)(a) or paragraph (5)(d), as applicable.

(c) An uninterrupted and unedited copy of the recording of the audio-video communication in which an online notarization is performed.

(7) Except as set forth in s. 709.2202, an act of witnessing performed pursuant to this section satisfies any requirement that the witness must be a subscribing or attesting witness or must be in the presence of the principal at the time of signing.

(8) The law of this state governs the validity of witnessing supervised by an online notary public pursuant to this section, regardless of the physical location of the witness at the time of witnessing. State and federal courts in this state have subject matter jurisdiction over any dispute arising out of an act of witnessing pursuant to this section, and may issue subpoenas for records or to require the appearance of witnesses in relation thereto in accordance with applicable law.

117.295 Standards for electronic and online notarization; rulemaking authority. —

(1) For purposes of this part, the Department of State may adopt rules necessary to implement the requirements of this chapter and to set standards for online notarization which include, but are not limited to:

(a) Improvements in technology and methods of assuring the identity of principals and the security of an electronic record, including tamper-evident technologies in compliance with the standards adopted pursuant to s. 117.021 which apply to online notarizations.

(b) Education requirements for online notaries public and the required terms of bonds and errors and omissions insurance, but not including the amounts of such bonds and insurance policies.

(c) Identity proofing, credential analysis, unauthorized interception, remote presentation, audio-video communication technology, and retention of electronic journals and copies of audio-video communications recordings in a secure repository.

(2) The Department of State shall:

(a) Adopt forms, processes, and rules necessary to accept applications from and register online notaries public pursuant to s. 117.225.

(b) Publish on its website a list containing each online notary public, the online notary public's RON service providers from January 1, 2022, and thereafter, the effective dates during which the online notary public used each RON service provider, as identified pursuant to ss. 117.225(5) and 117.265(5)(b), any secure repositories to which the online notary public may have delegated his or her duties pursuant to s. 117.245(4) from January 1, 2022, and thereafter, and the effective dates of that delegation.

(3) Until such time as the Department of State adopts rules setting standards that are equally or more protective, the following minimum standards shall apply to any online notarization performed by an online notary public of this state or his or her RON service provider:

(a) Use of identity proofing by means of knowledge-based authentication which must have, at a minimum, the following security characteristics:

1. The principal must be presented with five or more questions with a minimum of five possible answer choices per question.

2. Each question must be drawn from a third party provider of public and proprietary data sources and be identifiable to the principal's social security number or other identification information, or the principal's identity and historical events records.

3. Responses to all questions must be made within a 2-minute time constraint.

4. The principal must answer a minimum of 80 percent of the questions correctly.

5. The principal may be offered one additional attempt in the event of a failed attempt.

6. During the second attempt, the principal may not be presented with more than three questions from the prior attempt.

(b) Use of credential analysis using one or more commercially available automated software or hardware processes that are consistent with sound commercial practices; that aid the notary public in verifying the authenticity of the credential by analyzing the integrity of visual, physical, or cryptographic security features to indicate that the credential is not fraudulent or inappropriately modified; and that use information held or published by the issuing source or authoritative source, as available, to confirm the validity of credential details. The output of the credential analysis process must be provided to the online notary public performing the notarial act.

(c) Use of audio-video communication technology in completing online notarizations that must meet the following requirements:

1. The signal transmission must be reasonably secure from interception, access, or viewing by anyone other than the participants communicating.

2. The technology must provide sufficient audio clarity and video resolution to enable the notary to communicate with the principal and any witness, and to confirm the identity of the principal and any witness, as required, using the identification methods described in s. 117.265.

(4)(a) A RON service provider must file a self-certification with the Department of State, on a form adopted by department rule, confirming that its audio-video communication technology and related processes, services, software, data storage, or other services provided to online notaries public for the purpose of directly facilitating their performance of online notarizations satisfy the requirements of this chapter and any rules adopted by the Department of State pursuant to this section. Each certification shall remain active for a period of 1 year after the date of filing. The Department of

State must publish on its website a list of each RON service provider that has filed a self certification, the date of filing of the self-certification, any secure repositories to which the RON service provider may have delegated its duties pursuant to s. 117.245(4) from January 1, 2022, and thereafter, and the effective dates of that delegation.

(b) A RON service provider is deemed to have satisfied tamper-evident technology requirements by use of technology that renders any subsequent change or modification to the electronic record evident.

(5) In addition to any coverage it elects to provide for individual online notaries public, maintenance of errors and omissions insurance coverage by a RON service provider in a total amount of at least $250,000 in the annual aggregate with respect to potential errors or omissions in or relating to the technology or processes provided by the RON service provider. An online notary public is not responsible for the security of the systems used by the principal or others to access the online notarization session.

(6) A 2-hour in-person or online course addressing the duties, obligations, and technology requirements for serving as an online notary public offered by the Florida Land Title Association; the Real Property, Probate and Trust Law Section of the Florida Bar; the Florida Legal Education Association, Inc.; the Department of State; or a vendor approved by the Department of State shall satisfy the education requirements of s. 117.225(2). Each such provider shall make the in-person or online course generally available to all applicants. Regardless of membership in the provider's organization, the provider shall charge each attendee the same cost for the course unless the course is provided in conjunction with a regularly scheduled meeting of the provider's membership.

(7) The rulemaking required under this section is exempt from s. 120.541(3).

(8) A RON service provider may not use, sell, or offer to sell or transfer to another person for use or sale any personal information obtained under this part which identifies a principal, a witness, or a person named in a record presented for online notarization, except:

(a) As necessary to facilitate performance of a notarial act;

(b) To administer or process a record provided by or on behalf of a principal or the transaction of which the record is a part;

(c) To detect fraud, identity theft, or other criminal activities;

(d) In accordance with this part and the rules adopted pursuant to this part or any other applicable federal, state, or local law, or to comply with a lawful subpoena or court order or a lawful request from a law enforcement or regulatory agency;

(e) To monitor and improve the audio-video communication technology and related processes, services, software, data storage, or other services offered by the RON service provider to online notaries public for the purpose of directly facilitating their performance of online notarizations; or

(f) In connection with a proposed or actual sale, merger, transfer, or exchange of all or a portion of a business or operating unit of a RON service provider, or the dissolution, insolvency, or cessation of operations of a business or operating unit, if limited to such personal information held by that business or unit and any transferee agrees to comply with the restrictions set forth in this subsection.

117.305 Relation to federal law. — This part supersedes the Electronic Signatures in Global and National Commerce Act as authorized under 15 U.S.C. ss. 7001 et seq., but does not modify, limit, or supersede s. 101(c) of that act, 15 U.S.C. s. 7001(c), or authorize the electronic delivery of the notices described in 15 U.S.C. s. 7003(b).

CHAPTER 118. INTERNATIONAL NOTARIES

118.10 Civil-law notary.—

(1) As used in this section, the term:

(a) "Authentic act" means an instrument executed by a civil-law notary referencing this section, which instrument includes the particulars and capacities to act of any transacting parties, a confirmation of the full text of any necessary instrument, the signatures or their legal equivalent of any transacting parties, the signature and seal of a civil-law notary, and such other information prescribed by the Secretary of State.

(b) "Civil-law notary" means a person who is a member in good standing of The Florida Bar, who has practiced law for at least 5 years, and who is appointed by the Secretary of State as a civil-law notary.

(c) "Protocol" means a registry maintained by a civil-law notary in which the acts of the civil-law notary are archived.

(2) The Secretary of State shall have the power to appoint civil-law notaries and administer this section.

(3) A civil-law notary is authorized to issue authentic acts and thereby may authenticate or certify any document, transaction, event, condition, or occurrence. The contents of an authentic act and matters incorporated therein shall be presumed correct. A civil-law notary may also administer an oath and make a certificate thereof when it is necessary for execution of any writing or document to be attested, protested, or published under the seal of a notary public. A civil-law notary may also take acknowledgments of deeds and other instruments of writing for record, and solemnize the rites of matrimony, as fully as other officers of this state. A civil-law notary is not authorized to issue authentic acts for use in a jurisdiction if the United States Department of State has determined that the jurisdiction does not have diplomatic relations with the United States or is a terrorist country, or if trade with the jurisdiction is prohibited under the Trading With the Enemy Act of 1917, as amended, 50 U.S.C. ss. 1, et seq.

(4) The authentic acts, oaths and acknowledgments, and solemnizations of a civil-law notary shall be recorded in the civil-law notary's protocol in a manner prescribed by the Secretary of State.

(5) The Secretary of State may adopt rules prescribing:

(a) The form and content of authentic acts, oaths, acknowledgments, solemnizations, and signatures and seals or their legal equivalents;

(b) Procedures for the permanent archiving of authentic acts, maintaining records of acknowledgments, oaths and solemnizations, and procedures for the administration of oaths and taking of acknowledgments;

(c) The charging of reasonable fees to be retained by the Secretary of State for the purpose of administering this chapter;

(d) Educational requirements and procedures for testing applicants' knowledge of all matters relevant to the appointment, authority, duties or legal or ethical responsibilities of a civil-law notary;

(e) Procedures for the disciplining of civil-law notaries, including, but not limited to, the suspension and revocation of appointments for failure to comply with the requirements of this chapter or the rules of the Department of State, or for misrepresentation or fraud regarding the civil-law notary's authority, the effect of the civil-law notary's authentic acts, or the identities or acts of the parties to a transaction;

(f) Bonding or errors and omissions insurance requirements, or both, for civil-law notaries; and

(g) Other matters necessary for administering this section.

(6) The Secretary of State shall not regulate, discipline, or attempt to discipline any civil-law notary for, or with regard to, any action or conduct that would constitute the practice of law in this state, except by agreement with The Florida Bar. The Secretary of State shall not establish as a prerequisite to the appointment of a civil-law notary any test containing any question that inquires of the applicant's knowledge regarding the practice of law in the United States, unless such test is offered in conjunction with an educational program approved by The Florida Bar for continuing legal education credit.

(7) The powers of civil-law notaries include, but are not limited to, all of the powers of a notary public under any law of this state.

(8) This section shall not be construed as abrogating the provisions of any other act relating to notaries public, attorneys, or the practice of law in this state.

118.12 Certification of civil-law notary's authority; apostilles.—

If certification of a civil-law notary's authority is necessary for a particular document or transaction, it must be obtained from the Secretary of State. Upon the receipt of a written request from a civil-law notary and the fee prescribed by the Secretary of State, the Secretary of State shall issue a certification of the civil-law notary's authority, in a form prescribed by the Secretary of State, which shall include a statement explaining the legal qualifications and authority of a civil-law notary in this state. The fee prescribed for the issuance of the certification under this section or an apostille under s. 15.16 may not exceed $10 per document. The Department of State may adopt rules to implement this section. collector.

TITLE XXXIX. COMMERCIAL RELATIONS
CHAPTER 668. ELECTRONIC COMMERCE
PART II. UNIFORM ELECTRONIC TRANSACTIONS ACT

668.50 Uniform Electronic Transaction Act. —

(11) NOTARIZATION AND ACKNOWLEDGMENT.—

(a) If a law requires a signature or record to be notarized, acknowledged, verified, or made under oath, the requirement is satisfied if the electronic signature of the person authorized by applicable law to perform those acts, together with all other information required to be included by other applicable law, is attached to or logically associated with the signature or record. Neither a rubber stamp nor an impression type seal is required for an electronic notarization.

(b) A first-time applicant for a notary commission must submit proof that the applicant has, within 1 year prior to the application, completed at least 3 hours of interactive or classroom instruction, including electronic notarization, and covering the duties of the notary public. Courses satisfying this section may be offered by any public or private sector person or entity registered with the Executive Office of the Governor and must include a core curriculum approved by that office.

TITLE XL. REAL AND PERSONAL PROPERTY
CHAPTER 689. CONVEYANCES OF LAND AND DECLARATIONS OF TRUST

689.01 How real estate conveyed.—

(1) No estate or interest of freehold, or for a term of more than 1 year, or any uncertain interest of, in or out of any messuages, lands, tenements or hereditaments shall be created, made, granted, transferred or released in any other manner than by instrument in writing, signed in the presence of two subscribing witnesses by the party creating, making, granting, conveying, transferring or releasing such estate, interest, or term of more than 1 year, or by the party's lawfully authorized agent, unless by will and testament, or other testamentary appointment, duly made according to law; and no estate or interest, either of freehold, or of term of more than 1 year, or any uncertain interest of, in, to, or out of any messuages, lands, tenements or hereditaments, shall be assigned or surrendered unless it be by instrument signed in the presence of two subscribing witnesses by the party so assigning or surrendering, or by the party's lawfully authorized agent, or by the act and operation of law. No seal shall be necessary to give validity to any instrument executed in conformity with this section. Corporations may execute any and all conveyances in accordance with the provisions of this section or ss. 692.01 and 692.02.

(2) For purposes of this chapter:

(a) Any requirement that an instrument be signed in the presence of two subscribing witnesses may be satisfied by witnesses being present and electronically signing by means of audio-video communication technology, as defined in s. 117.201.

(b) The act of witnessing an electronic signature is satisfied if a witness is in the physical presence of the principal or present through audio-video communication technology at the time the principal affixes his or her electronic signature and the witness hears the principal make a statement acknowledging that the principal has signed the electronic record.

(c) The terms used in this subsection have the same meanings as the terms defined in s. 117.201.

(3) All acts of witnessing made or taken in the manner described in subsection (2) are validated and, upon recording, may not be denied to have provided constructive notice based on any alleged failure to have strictly complied with this section or the laws governing notarization of instruments, including online notarization. This subsection does not preclude a challenge to the validity or enforceability of an instrument or electronic record based upon fraud, forgery, impersonation, duress, incapacity, undue influence, minority, illegality, unconscionability, or any other basis not related to the act of witnessing.

CHAPTER 695. RECORD OF CONVEYANCES OF REAL ESTATE

695.03 Acknowledgment and proof; validation of certain acknowledgments; legalization or authentication before foreign officials. — To entitle any instrument concerning real property to be recorded, the execution must be acknowledged by the party executing it, proved by a subscribing witness to it, or legalized or authenticated in one of the following forms:

(1) WITHIN THIS STATE.-An acknowledgment or proof may be taken, administered, or made within this state by or before a judge, clerk, or deputy clerk of any court; a United States commissioner or magistrate; or a notary public or civil-law notary of this state, and the certificate of acknowledgment or proof must be under the seal of the court or officer, as the case may be.

(2) OUTSIDE THIS STATE BUT WITHIN THE UNITED STATES.- An acknowledgment or a proof taken, administered, or made outside of this state but within the United

States may be taken, administered, or made by or before a civil-law notary of this state or a commissioner of deeds appointed by the Governor of this state; a judge or clerk of any court of the United States or of any state, territory, or district; by or before a United States commissioner or magistrate; or by or before any notary public, justice of the peace, master in chancery, or registrar or recorder of deeds of any state, territory, or district having a seal, and the certificate of acknowledgment or proof must be under the seal of the court or officer, as the case may be. If the acknowledgment or proof is taken, administered, or made before a notary public who does not affix a seal, it is sufficient for the notary public to type, print, or write by hand on the instrument,

> "I am a Notary Public of the State of _____ (state), and my commission expires on _____ (date)."

(3) OUTSIDE OF THE UNITED STATES OR WITHIN FOREIGN COUNTRIES.—

An acknowledgment, an affidavit, an oath, a legalization, an authentication, or a proof taken, administered, or made outside of the United States or in a foreign country may be taken, administered, or made by or before a commissioner of deeds appointed by the Governor of this state to act in such country; before a notary public of such foreign country or a civil-law notary of this state or of such foreign country who has an official seal; before an ambassador, envoy extraordinary, minister plenipotentiary, minister, commissioner, charge d'affaires, consul general, consul, vice consul, consular agent, or other diplomatic or consular officer of the United States appointed to reside in such country; or before a military or naval officer authorized by 10 U.S.C. s. 1044a to perform the duties of notary public, and the certificate of acknowledgment, legalization, authentication, or proof must be under the seal of the officer. A certificate legalizing or authenticating the signature of a person executing an instrument concerning real property and to which a civil-law notary or notary public of that country has affixed her or his official seal is sufficient as an acknowledgment. For the purposes of this section, the term "civil-law notary" means a civil-law notary as defined in chapter 118 or an official of a foreign country who has an official seal and who is authorized to make legal or lawful the execution of any document in that jurisdiction, in which jurisdiction the affixing of her or his official seal is deemed proof of the execution of the document or deed in full compliance with the laws of that jurisdiction.

(4) COMPLIANCE AND VALIDATION.—The affixing of the official seal or the electronic equivalent thereof under s. 117.021 or other applicable law, including part II of chapter 117, conclusively establishes that the acknowledgment or proof was taken, administered, or made in full compliance with the laws of this state or, as applicable, the laws of the other state, or of the foreign country governing notarial acts. All affidavits, oaths, acknowledgments, legalizations, authentications, or proofs taken, administered, or made in any manner as set forth in subsections (1), (2), and (3) are validated and upon recording may not be denied to have provided constructive notice based on any alleged failure to have strictly complied with this section, as currently or previously in effect, or the laws governing notarization of instruments.

This subsection does not preclude a challenge to the validity or enforceability of an instrument or electronic record based upon fraud, forgery, impersonation, duress, incapacity, undue influence, minority, illegality, unconscionability, or any other basis not related to the notarial act or constructive notice provided by recording.

695.031 Affidavits and acknowledgments by members of armed forces and their spouses.—

(1) In addition to the manner, form and proof of acknowledgment of instruments as

now provided by law, any person serving in or with the Armed Forces of the United States, including the Army, Navy, Marine Corps, Coast Guard, or any component or any arm or service of any thereof, including any female auxiliary of any thereof, and any person whose duties require his or her presence with the Armed Forces of the United States, as herein designated, or otherwise designated by law or military or naval command, may acknowledge any instrument, wherever located, either within or without the state, or without the United States, before any commissioned officer in active service of the Armed Forces of the United States, as herein designated, or otherwise designated by law, or military or naval command, or order, with the rank of second lieutenant or higher in the Army or Marine Corps, or of any component or any arm or service of either thereof, including any female auxiliary of any thereof, or ensign or higher in the Navy or United States Coast Guard, or of any component or any arm or service of either thereof, including any female auxiliary of any thereof.

(2) The instrument shall not be rendered invalid by the failure to state therein the place of execution or acknowledgment. No authentication of the officer's certificate of acknowledgment or otherwise shall be required, and no seal shall be necessary, but the officer taking the acknowledgment shall endorse thereon or attach thereto a certificate substantially in the following form:

> On this _____ day of _____, (year), before me _____, the undersigned officer, personally appeared _____, known to me (or satisfactorily proven) to be serving in or with, or whose duties require her or his presence with the Armed Forces of the United States, and to be the person whose name is subscribed to the within instrument, and acknowledged that she or he executed the same for the purposes therein contained, and the undersigned does further certify that she or he is at the date of this certificate a commissioned officer of the rank stated below and is in the active service of the Armed Forces of the United States.
>
> (Signature of commissioned officer.)
> (Rank of commissioned officer and command or branch of service to which officer is attached.)

695.25 Short form of acknowledgment.—

The forms of acknowledgment set forth in this section may be used, and are sufficient for their respective purposes, under any law of this state. The forms shall be known as "Statutory Short Forms of Acknowledgment" and may be referred to by that name. The authorization of the forms in this section does not preclude the use of other forms.

(1) For an individual acting in his or her own right:

> STATE OF _____
> COUNTY OF _____
>
> The foregoing instrument was acknowledged before me by means of [ ] physical presence or [ ] online notarization, this _____ (date) by _____ (name of person acknowledging), who is personally known to me or who has produced _____ (type of identification) as identification.
>
> (Signature of person taking acknowledgment)
> (Name typed, printed or stamped)
> (Title or rank)
> (Serial number, if any)

(2) For a corporation:

STATE OF _____
COUNTY OF _____

The foregoing instrument was acknowledged before me by means of [ ] physical presence or [ ] online notarization, this _____ (date) by _____ (name of officer or agent, title of officer or agent) of _____ (name of corporation acknowledging), a _____ (state or place of incorporation) corporation, on behalf of the corporation. He/she is personally known to me or has produced _____ (type of identification) as identification.

(Signature of person taking acknowledgment)
(Name typed, printed or stamped)
(Title or rank)
(Serial number, if any)

(3) For a limited liability company:

STATE OF _____
COUNTY OF _____

The foregoing instrument was acknowledged before me by means of [ ] physical presence or [ ] online notarization, this _____ (date) by _____ (name of member, manager, officer or agent, title of member, manager, officer or agent), of _____ (name of company acknowledging), a _____ (state or place of formation) limited liability company, on behalf of the company, who is personally known to me or has produced _____ (type of identification) as identification.

(Signature of person taking acknowledgment)
(Name typed, printed or stamped)

(4) For a partnership:

STATE OF _____
COUNTY OF _____

The foregoing instrument was acknowledged before me by means of [ ] physical presence or [ ] online notarization, this _____ (date) by _____ (name of acknowledging partner or agent), partner _____ (or agent) on behalf of _____ (name of partnership), a partnership. He/she is personally known to me or has produced _____ (type of identification) as identification.

(Signature of person taking acknowledgment)
(Name typed, printed or stamped)
(Title or rank)
(Serial number, if any)

(5) For an individual acting as principal by an attorney in fact:

STATE OF _____
COUNTY OF _____

The foregoing instrument was acknowledged before me by means of [ ] physical presence or [ ] online notarization, this _____ (date) by _____ (name of attorney in fact) as attorney in fact, who is personally known to me or who has produced _____ (type of identification) as identification on behalf of _____ (name of principal).

(Signature of person taking acknowledgment)
(Name typed, printed or stamped)
(Title or rank)
(Serial number, if any)

(6) By any public officer, trustee, or personal representative:

STATE OF _____
COUNTY OF _____

The foregoing instrument was acknowledged before me by means of [ ] physical presence or [ ] online notarization, this _____ (date) by _____ (name and title of position), who is personally known to me or who has produced _____ (type of identification) as identification.

(Signature of person taking acknowledgment)
(Name typed, printed or stamped)
(Title or rank)
(Serial number, if any)

695.26 Requirements for recording instruments affecting real property.—

*(1)(d) The name of any notary public or other officer authorized to take acknowledgments or proofs whose signature appears upon the instrument is legibly printed, typewritten, or stamped upon such instrument immediately beneath the signature of such notary public or other officer authorized to take acknowledgment or proofs.

*This is not the only recording requirement but it is the only one that is directly related to the notarization. This section does not apply to: documents executed before July 1, 1991: an instrument executed, acknowledged, or proved outside of the state: or a will. For a complete understanding of recording requirements, please review all of s.695.26, Florida Statutes, or contact the recording section of the county clerk's office.

CHAPTER 695 UNIFORM REAL PROPERTY ELECTRONIC RECORDING ACT

695.27 Uniform Real Property Electronic Recording Act.—

(3) VALIDITY OF ELECTRONIC DOCUMENTS.—

(a) If a law requires, as a condition for recording, that a document be an original, be on paper or another tangible medium, or be in writing, the requirement is satisfied by an electronic document satisfying the requirements of this section.

(b) If a law requires, as a condition for recording, that a document be signed, the requirement is satisfied by an electronic signature.

(c) A requirement that a document or a signature associated with a document be notarized, acknowledged, verified, witnessed, or made under oath is satisfied if the electronic signature of the person authorized to perform that act, and all other information required to be included, is attached to or logically associated with the document or signature. A physical or electronic image of a stamp, impression, or seal need not accompany an electronic signature.

TITLE XLII. ESTATES AND TRUSTS
CHAPTER 732. PROBATE CODE: INTESTATE SUCCESSION AND WILLS

732.503 Self-proof of will.—

(1) A will or codicil executed in conformity with s. 732.502 may be made self-proved at the time of its execution or at any subsequent date by the acknowledgment of it by the testator and the affidavits of the witnesses, made before an officer authorized to administer oaths and evidenced by the officer's certificate attached to or following the will, in substantially the following form:

STATE OF _____
COUNTY OF _____

I, _____, declare to the officer taking my acknowledgment of this instrument, and to the subscribing witnesses, that I signed this instrument as my will.
(Testator)

We, _____ and _____, have been sworn by the officer signing below, and declare to that officer on our oaths that the testator declared the instrument to be the testator's will and signed it in our presence and that we each signed the instrument as a witness in the presence of the testator and of each other.

(Signature of Testator)
(Signature of Witness)
(Signature of Witness)

Acknowledged and subscribed before me by means of ☐ physical presence or ☐ online notarization by the testator, (type or print testator's name), ☐ who is personally known to me or ☐ has produced (state type of identification--see s. 117.05(5)(b)2.) as identification, and sworn to and subscribed before me by each of the following witnesses:
(type or print name of first witness) who ☐ is personally known to me or ☐ has produced (state type of identification--see s. 117.05(5)(b)2.) as identification, by means of ☐ physical presence or ☐ online notarization; and (type or print name of second witness) who ☐ is personally known to me or ☐ has produced (state type of identification--see s. 117.05(5)(b)2.) as identification, by means of ☐ physical presence or ☐ online notarization. Subscribed by me in the presence of the testator and the subscribing witnesses, by the means specified herein, all on (date).

(Signature of Officer)
(Print, type, or stamp commissioned name of Notary Public)

(2) A will or codicil made self-proved under former law, or executed in another state and made self-proved under the laws of that state, shall be considered as self-proved under this section.

FLORIDIA ADMINISTRATIVE CODE

CHAPTER 1. DEPARTMENT OF STATE
CHAPTER 1N. DIVISION OF CORPORATIONS
CHAPTER 1N-5. ELECTRONIC NOTARIZATION

1N-5.001 Definitions.

(1) "Capable of independent verification" means any interested person may reasonably determine the notary's identity, the notary's relevant authority and that the electronic signature is the act of the particular notary identified by the signature.

(2) "Electronic document" means information that is created, generated, sent, communicated, received, or stored by electronic means.

(3) "Electronic notarization" and "electronic notarial act" means an official act authorized under Section 117.021(1), F.S., using electronic documents and electronic signatures.

(4) "Electronic Notary System" means a set of applications, programs, hardware, software, or technology designed to enable a notary to perform electronic notarizations.

(5) "Electronic signature" means an electronic sound, symbol, or process attached to or logically associated with an electronic document and executed or adopted by a person with the intent to sign the electronic document or record.

(6) "Attached to or logically associated with" means the notary's electronic signature is securely bound to the electronic document in such a manner as to make it impracticable to falsify or alter, without detection, either the signature or the document.

(7) "Unique to the notary public" means the notary's electronic signature is attributable solely to the notary public to the exclusion of all other persons.

(8) "Retained under the notary public's sole control" means accessible by and attributable solely to the notary to the exclusion of all other persons and entities, either through being in the direct physical custody of the notary or through being secured with one or more biometric, password, token, or other authentication technologies in an electronic notarization system that meets the performance requirements of Sections 117.021(2) and (3), F.S.

(9) "Public key certificate" means a computer-based record that:

(a) Identifies the certification authority issuing it;

(b) Names or identifies its subscriber;

(c) Contains the subscriber's public key; and

(d) Is digitally signed by the certification authority issuing it.

Rulemaking Authority 117.021(5) FS. Law Implemented 117.021 FS. History–New 1-26-10.

1N-5.002 Notary's Electronic Signature.

(1) In performing an electronic notarial act, a notary shall execute an electronic signature in a manner that attributes such signature to the notary public identified on the official commission.

(2) A notary shall take reasonable steps to ensure the security, reliability and uniformity of electronic notarizations, including, but not limited to, the use of an authentication procedure such as a password, token, card or biometric to protect access to the notary's electronic signature or the means for affixing the signature.

(3) The notary's electronic signature and seal information may be affixed by means of a public key certificate.

(4) The notary's electronic signature and seal information may be affixed by means of an electronic notary system.

(5) Any public key certificate or electronic notary system that is used to affix the Notary's electronic signature and seal information shall be issued at the third or higher level of assurance as defined by the U. S. National Institute of Standards and Technology (NIST) Special Publication 800-63(NIST800-63), Electronic Authentication Guideline Version 1.0.2., available at NIST's website www.csrc.nist.gov which is incorporated by reference at: https://www.flrules.org/Gateway/reference.asp?No=Ref-07017 and may be accessed at the following URL:

http://nvlpubs.nist.gov/nistpubs/SpecialPublications/NIST.SP.800-63-2.pdf.

Rulemaking Authority 117.021(5) FS. Law Implemented 117.021 FS. History–New 1-26-10, Amended 6-27-16.

CHAPTER 1N-6 FLORIDA CIVIL-LAW NOTARY

1N-6.001 Florida Civil-law Notary.

(1) Application:

(a) Florida Civil-law Notaries appointed pursuant to this rule may continue to use the title "Florida International Notary" wherever that title is used or required to be used under this rule. Persons wishing to be appointed by the Secretary of State as Florida Civil-law Notaries may request an application by writing to the following address and requesting Form Number DS-DE-38, titled "Application for Appointment as a Florida Civil-law Notary," Effective October 8, 1998, which form is hereby incorporated by reference. All other forms discussed in this rule may be obtained by writing the same address:

Department of State
Office of the Secretary
PL-02
The Capitol
Tallahassee, Florida 32399-0250

(b) The application to become a Florida Civil-law Notary must be complete and on the above form prescribed by the Department of State. The application must be accompanied by:

1. A certificate of good standing from the Supreme Court of Florida issued within 90 days of the date of application showing that the applicant is currently a member of the Florida Bar and has been a member of The Florida Bar for at least five years.

2. An application processing fee in the amount of fifty dollars.

(2) Educational programs:

(a) Persons or entities who wish to submit a proposed civil-law notary curriculum or course of study to the Department of State for consideration as to its acceptability by the Department of State may do so. Any such curriculum or course of study submitted for the Department of State's approval should incorporate all of the following elements:

1. The nature and characteristics of notarial practice in civil-law jurisdictions including a review of the historical development of civil-law notarial practice;

2. A comparison of notarial functions and the nature and characteristics of notarial practice under Chapter 117, F.S., and civil-law notarial functions and practices under Chapter 118, F.S., including a review of the historical development of common law notarial practice;

3. The nature and characteristics of the Florida Civil-law notary, including a

comparison of notarial practice in civil-law countries and practice as a non-lawyer notary public under Chapter 117, F.S.;

4. The similarities and differences between practicing as a Florida Civil-law Notary and the traditional practice of law in the State of Florida;

5. The purposes of and uses of authentic acts, and the rules regulating the execution of authentic acts, administration of oaths, and taking of acknowledgments by Florida Civil-law Notaries;

6. Solemnization of marriage by a Florida Civil-law Notary;

7. Florida laws relevant to practice as a Florida Civil-law Notary;

8. Rules regulating The Florida Bar including the Rules of Discipline and the Rules of Professional Conduct;

9. The potential malpractice liability of Florida Civil-law Notary.

(b) The Department of State shall maintain a list of the currently approved Florida Civil-law Notary education programs and shall make the list available upon request. Each education program shall be subject to annual renewal.

(c) Persons who have had a curriculum or course of study approved by the Department may also administer the Department's civil-law notary test under the Department's supervision, but may not charge a fee in excess of $200 to any person for administering a test to that person. All test materials are confidential property of the Department of State and any person who compromises the confidentiality of the test materials or allows another to do so shall not in the future be authorized by the Department to serve as a test administrator.

(3) Examination:

(a) A Florida Civil-law Notary application shall be valid for a period of one year from the date on which the application was received by the Department of State during which time the applicant must complete the Florida Civil-law Notary examination. If the applicant completes the examination, with a satisfactory score of 70%, within the one year period prescribed above, the applicant remains eligible for appointment as a Florida Civil-law Notary even though the appointment itself may occur more than one year after the date on which the application was received.

(b) After reviewing the application for completeness and accuracy of information, determining that all necessary documents accompany the application, and that the applicant meets the requirements of this rule and Section 118.10, F.S., the Department of State will provide the applicant with a certificate of eligibility to take the Florida Civillaw Notary examination and a list of examination dates and corresponding examination locations.

(c) The applicant who has been certified as eligible must notify the Department of State at least two weeks in advance of any scheduled examination that the applicant intends to take a scheduled examination. If notice is not received, or if the notice is untimely, the applicant will not be admitted to the examination.

(d) Upon appearing at the examination location, and prior to entering the examination facility, the applicant must present to the examination authorities the certificate of eligibility issued to the applicant by the Department of State, a governmentally issued identification card which bears the applicant's picture, and pay the examination fee.

(4) Appointment, Revocation, Voluntary Resignation:

(a) Upon completion of each examination session and after the examinations are scored, the testing authority shall promptly forward the examination results to the

Department of State. The Department of State shall then notify the applicants of their respective test scores and shall appoint those persons with satisfactory scores of 70% as Florida Civil-law Notaries.

(b) Upon accepting appointment as a Florida Civil-law Notary, the applicant shall file within 90 days after appointment with the Department of State Form Number DS-DE-42, titled "Appointment of Protocol Custodian and Seal Filing," Effective October 8, 1998, which form is hereby incorporated herein by reference. The applicant shall identify a Florida Civil-law Notary in good standing with the Department of State and The Florida Bar who has agreed to take custody of the applicant's protocol in the event that the applicant's appointment is ever suspended or revoked, or if the applicant dies or becomes incapacitated. If for any reason a Florida Civil-law Notary chooses to change secondary custodial notaries, the Florida Civil-law Notary shall promptly notify the Department of State in writing and shall make the appropriate change in the civil-law notary's annual report.

(c) Unless suspended or revoked in accordance with this rule, an appointment as a Florida Civil-law Notary shall continue in force for so long as the applicant is a member in good standing of The Florida Bar, subject to the requirement that the applicant must file an annual report with the Florida Department of State at the address noted above on Form Number DS-DE-39, titled "Florida Civil-law Notary Annual Report," effective October 8, 1998, which form is hereby incorporated by reference. The annual report shall include the civil-law notary's current business address and telephone number and the identity and signature of another Florida Civil-law Notary who has agreed to take custody of the civil-law notary's protocol upon the suspension, revocation, incapacitation or death of the civil-law notary. A processing fee payable to the Department of State in the amount of fifty dollars shall accompany the annual report. Failure to file an annual report with the Florida Department of State shall result in revocation of the civil-law notary's appointment.

(5) Form and content of signatures and seals; registration of signatures and seals:

(a) A Florida Civil-law Notary's original hand written signature and seal shall be registered with the Department of State. No Florida Civil-law Notary shall take any official action or execute any document as a civil-law notary until his seal has properly registered.

(b) Except for those documents executed by digital signature as provided under subparagraph (6)(b)2. this rule, the Florida Civil-law Notary's original handwritten signature and an original rubber stamp or embossed impression of the civil-law notary's seal shall be affixed by the civil-law notary to all documents executed by the civil-law notary while acting in as a Florida Civil-law Notary under Chapter 118, F.S.. The civillaw notary shall not allow any other person to sign or seal a document using the civil-law notary's official signature or seal.

(c) The civil-law notary's seal may be an embossing seal or a rubber stamp and may be circular or square in shape and shall not be more than two inches nor less than one inch in diameter if circular, or more than two inches on each side nor less than one inch on each side if square.

(d) A registered signature and seal may be changed by applying to the Department of State at the address listed above for Form Number DS-DE-41, Effective October 8, 1998, which form is hereby incorporated herein by reference. An application to change a signature or seal shall be considered an amendment to the notary's application and shall be accompanied by a processing fee of $25.00.

(6)(a) Form and content of authentic acts:(b) Each authentic act shall contain:

1. The handwritten signature and original seal of the Florida Civil-law Notary.

2. The signature and seal may be incorporated into public key certificate which complies with the requirements of Rule 1-10.001, F.A.C. When serving as part of an authentication instrument, the public key certificate of a Florida Civil-law Notary must clearly show the Florida Civil-law Notary's signature and seal are registered with the Department of State.

3. The typewritten full name of the Florida Civil-law Notary in the form in which the notary's application for appointment was originally submitted to the Department of State and the words "Florida Civil-law Notary" typewritten in the English language.

4. The current business address and telephone number of the Florida Civil-law Notary typewritten in the English language.

5. A statement typewritten in the English language that "Under the laws of the State of Florida, Section 118.10, F.S., this authentic act is legally equivalent to the authentic acts of civil-law notaries in all jurisdictions outside the geographic borders of the United States and is issued on the authority of the Florida Secretary of State."

6. The date on which the authentic act was signed and sealed by the Florida Civil-law Notary and the signatures of the parties to the transaction.

7. All words or statements required to appear in the English language may also appear in any other language.

8. An authentic act may also contain such other information or material as may be required to satisfy any legal requirements, or to satisfy ethical or legal concerns, or the business needs of the parties to the transaction or of the Florida Civil-law Notary including statements attesting to the signatures on accompanying documents if executed in the Florida Civil-law Notary's presence, and any witnessing signatures; a statement confirming the legality of the transaction and the contents of any documents and any limitations thereon; any facts contained in the documents or relied on by any interested party and any limitations thereon.

(7) Procedures for the administration of oaths; taking of acknowledgments and solemnizations of marriage:

(a) A Florida Civil-law Notary may administer an oath and make a certificate thereof when it is necessary for the execution of any writing or document to be attested, protested, or published under seal of a notary public. In administering the oath, the Florida Civil-law Notary must require the signer to voluntarily swear or affirm that the statements contained in the documents are true.

(b) A Florida Civil-law Notary may administer an acknowledgment of deeds and other instruments of writing for record. Such acknowledgment does not require that an oath be taken, but the signer must acknowledge that the execution of the document is his or her voluntary act. The Florida Civil-law Notary may not take an acknowledgment of execution in lieu of an oath if an oath is required.

(c) A Florida Civil-law Notary may not administer an oath to a person or take his or her acknowledgment unless he or she personally knows, as defined in Section 117.05(5)(a), F.S., or has satisfactory evidence, as defined in Section 117.05(5)(b), F.S., that the person whose oath is to be administered or whose acknowledgment is to be taken, is the individual who is described in and who is executing the authentic act or other instrument. A Florida Civil-law Notary may not administer an oath to a person or take his or her acknowledgment unless the person whose oath is being administered or whose acknowledgment is to be taken is in the presence of the Florida Civil-law Notary at the time the oath is being administered or the acknowledgment is being taken.

(d) An oath or acknowledgment taken or administered by a Florida Civil-law Notary shall be signed in the presence of the notary, and where otherwise required by law witnessed in the presence of the Florida Civil-law Notary, and shall be executed with the civil-law notary's handwritten signature and original seal.

(e) A Florida Civil-law Notary may use any of the forms prescribed in Chapter 117, F.S., for administering oaths or taking acknowledgments but shall not be required to do so, and an oath or acknowledgment may be, but is not required to be, incorporated into any document executed by a civil-law notary as an authentic act. This section does relieve the civil-law notary of the obligation to secure the signatures of other witnesses where otherwise required by law.

(8) The Florida Civil-law Notary's Protocol:

(a) A Florida Civil-law Notary's protocol shall be maintained in a secure, fireproof location at the Florida Civil-law Notary's principal place of business;

(b) The protocol shall contain an original copy or photocopy of each of the Florida Civil-law Notary's authentic acts in date sequence, and an original photocopy of any supporting or related documents, which shall be permanently archived in the protocol.

The protocol shall also contain, in date sequence, a photocopy or original copy of any document containing, incorporating or depending upon, an acknowledgment, oath or solemnization executed by the civil-law notary, which shall include a copy of any certificate made by the civil-law notary.

(c) The protocol shall contain or be accompanied by an index to its contents in date order. In addition to the date on which act, oath, acknowledgment, or solemnization was executed, each entry in the index shall identify the party or parties who paid the notary's fee.

(d) The protocol shall be available for inspection by the Department of State during reasonable business hours and copies of any documents contained in the protocol shall be furnished to the Department upon request. The contents of the protocol shall otherwise be considered confidential and shall be made available only to persons who have a legal interest in a particular transaction.

(e) A Florida Civil-law Notary who takes custody of the protocol of another Florida Civil-law Notary's protocol because of suspension or incapacitation shall maintain the protocol until the suspension period expires or the incapacitation is relieved. When a Florida Civil-law Notary takes custody of another Florida Civil-law Notary's protocol because of revocation or death the custodial Florida Civil-law Notary shall permanently maintain the protocol in accordance with this rule.

(9) Discipline; suspension and revocation:

(a) A Florida Civil-law Notary shall be disciplined for violation of this rule. All complaints to the Department of State concerning the conduct or acts of a Florida Civillaw Notary will also be referred to The Florida Bar for a determination by the Bar as to whether the complaint alleges a violation of the rules of The Florida Bar governing the conduct and discipline of lawyers.

(b) All complaints to the Department of State concerning the conduct or acts of a Florida Civil-law Notary which on their face appear to establish facts which if proven true would constitute an act of misrepresentation or fraud in the creation or execution of an authentication instrument will be investigated by the Department of State to determine whether cause exists to suspend the Florida Civil-law Notary's appointment or reprimand the Florida Civil-law Notary.

(c) After investigation and upon a determination by the Department that one or more acts of misrepresentation, fraud or violation of this rule has been committed by a

Florida Civil-law Notary, the Department of State shall, after considering the extent of the fraud or misrepresentation including the number of persons involved and the effect on those persons; the number of acts of misrepresentation or fraud; any financial loss or other injury that may have resulted; and the degree of culpability of the Florida Civil-law Notary:

1. Issue a letter of warning to the Florida Civil-law Notary including the Department's findings;

2. Order compliance with this rule;

3. Order restitution;

4. Order suspension of the appointment of the Florida Civil-law Notary;

5. Order revocation of the appointment of the Florida Civil-law Notary.

(d) Any order under this rule which requires payment of restitution or results in the suspension or revocation of the appointment of a Florida Civil-law Notary shall be accompanied by a notice of final agency action as required by Chapter 120, F.S., and the Florida Civil-law Notary shall be entitled to a hearing in accordance with the requirements of Sections 120.57 and 120.569, F.S.

(e) A former Florida Civil-law Notary whose appointment has been finally revoked shall not be eligible to apply for a new appointment as a Florida Civil-law Notary for a period of at least five years.

(f) A Florida Civil-law Notary may voluntarily resign from an appointment by notifying the Department of State in writing at the above address of the intention to do so.

Any voluntary resignation from an appointment as a Florida Civil-law Notary shall be permanent and the resigned Florida Civil-law Notary may only resume service as a Florida Civil-law Notary after successfully completing a new application and examination process.

Rulemaking Authority 118.10(5) FS. Law Implemented 118.10 FS. History — New 6-15-98, Amended 10-8-98, Formerly 1C-18.001.

CHAPTER 1N-7. REMOTE ONLINE NOTARIZATION

1N-7.001 Remote Online Notarization

(1) Words and terms defined in Section 117.201, F.S., shall have the same meaning in this chapter. For the purpose of this chapter the following words and terms shall have the following meanings, unless the context clearly indicates otherwise:

(a) "Registrant" means any person registering applying as for an online public notary pursuant to Section 117.225, F.S.

(b) "Attached to or logically associated with" means the notary's electronic signature is securely bound to the electronic document in such a manner as to make it impracticable to falsify or alter, without detection, either the signature or the document.

(c) "Department" means the Florida Department of State.

(d) "Electronic document" means information that is created, generated, sent, communicated, received, or stored by electronic means.

(e) "Electronic notarization" and "electronic notarial act" means an official act authorized under Section 117.021(1), F.S., using electronic documents and electronic signatures.

(f) "Electronic Notary System" means a set of applications, programs, hardware, software, or technology designed to enable a notary to perform electronic notarizations.

(g) "Electronic signature" means an electronic sound, symbol, or process attached to or logically associated with an electronic document and executed or adopted by a person with the intent to sign the electronic document or record.

(h) "Unique to the notary public" means the notary's electronic signature is attributable solely to the notary public to the exclusion of all other persons.

(i) "Retained under the online notary public's sole control" means accessible by and attributable solely to the notary to the exclusion of all other persons and entities, either through being in the direct physical custody of the notary or through being secured with one or more biometric, password, token, or other authentication technologies in an electronic notarization system that meets the performance requirements of Sections 117.021(2) and (3), F.S.

(j) "Tamper-evident technology" means technology that allows a person inspecting a record to determine whether there has been any tampering with the integrity of a certificate of electronic notarial act logically associated with a record or with the attachment or association of the notarial act with that electronic document.

(2) A registrant shall submit form DOC 1N7(http://www.flrules.org/Gateway/reference.asp?No=Ref-11541), effective 01/2020 herein incorporated by reference.

(3) The registrant shall:

(a) Submit a payment registration fee of $10 by check payable to the Florida Department of State; and

(b) Submit the application by:

1. U.S. mail to P.O. Box 6327, Tallahassee, FL 32314;

2. In person delivery; or

3. Courier service.

4. In person delivery and courier service will go to 2415 North Monroe St., Suite 810, Tallahassee 32303.

(4) A registration is effective upon filing by the Florida Department State and expires on the date of expiration, termination, or resignation of the registrant's:

(a) Notary Public commission issued under Section 117.01, F.S.;

(b) Appointment as a civil-law Notary pursuant to Section 118.10, F.S., and Chapter 1N-5, F.A.C.; or

(c) Appointment as a commissioner of deeds pursuant to Section 721.97, F.S.

(5) All qualifications and registration requirements applicable for an applicant's registration shall apply to a renewal registration

(6) The online notary public's electronic journal, electronic signature, and electronic seal shall be retained under the online notary public's sole control. The online notary public may not allow another person to use the online notary public's electronicjournal, electronic signature, or electronic seal.

(7) An online notary public shall attach the online notary public's electronic signature and seal to the electronic notarial certificate of an electronic document in a manner that is capable of independent verification and renders any subsequent change or modification to the electronic document evident.

(8) Online notaries public shall utilize remote online notary service providers to facilitate their performance of online notarization.

(9) The remote online service provider utilized by the online notaries public shall comply with the standards and requirements pursuant to Section 117.295, F.S., and utilize tamper-evident technologies.

Rulemaking Authority 117.295 FS. Law Implemented 117.225, 117.295 FS. History–New 2-16-20.

1N-7.005 Online Notary Public and RON Service Provider Required Information.

(1) Online notary public.

(a) Within 30 day of the effective date of this rule, a currently registered online notary public shall provide the Florida Department of State the name of the online notary public's RON service providers, the effective dates during which the online notary public used each RON service provider, and, if applicable, the name of any secured repositories to which the online notary public may have delegated his or her duties pursuant to Section 117.245(4), F.S., from January 1, 2022, and thereafter.

(b) An individual registering as an online notary public, shall provide this information at the time of his or her registration.

(c) The online notary public shall submit this information on Form Number DS-DOC50, titled "Online Notary Public: Required Information," Effective 02/2022, which form is hereby incorporated by reference and is available on the Department of State's website at https://dos.myflorida.com/sunbiz/other-services/notaries/notary-forms/ or http://www.flrules.org/Gateway/reference.asp?No=Ref-14032.

(d) An online notary public that changes, adds, or removes a RON service provider or secured repository from the online notary public's use shall submit to the Department within 30 days of the change an amended Form DS-DOC-50 identifying the online notary public's updated RON service providers and, if applicable, secured repositories.

(2) RON service provider.

(a) Within 30 day of the effective date of this rule, and annually thereafter, a RON service provider shall provide the Florida Department of State, a self-certification form confirming that its audio-video communication technology and related processes, services software, data storage, or other services provided to online notaries public for the performance of online notarization satisfy the requirements of Chapter 117, F.S., and any rules promulgated by the Florida Department of State pursuant to Section 117.295, F.S.

(b) The RON service provider's self-certification is effective for a period of 1 year after the date the RON service provider files it with the Department.

(c) If applicable, the RON service provider shall, at the same time it files its self certification, identify any secure repositories to which the RON service provider may have delegated its duties pursuant to Section 117.245(4), F.S., from January 1, 2022, and thereafter.

(d) The RON service provider shall submit this information on Form Number DSDOC-51, titled "RON Service Provider: Self-Certification and Required Information," Effective 02/2022, which form is hereby incorporated by reference and is available on the Department of State's website at https://dos.myflorida.com/sunbiz/other-services/notaries/notary-forms/ or http://www.flrules.org/Gateway/reference.asp?No=Ref-14033.

(e) A RON service provider that, pursuant to Section 117.245(4), F.S., delegates its duties to a secured repository after it has already filed its annual certification shall submit to the Department an amended Form DS-DOC-51 within 30 days after making such delegation.

(f) An entity that seeks to begin providing RON service provider functions after the effective date of this rule shall submit the information required by this section prior to providing RON service provider functions.

Rulemaking Authority 117.295 FS. Law Implemented 117.245, 117.295 FS. History–New 2-22-22. ■

About the NNA

Since 1957, the National Notary Association has been committed to serving and educating the nation's Notaries. During that time, the NNA® has become known as the most trusted source of information for and about Notaries and Notary laws, rules and best practices.

The NNA serves Notaries through its NationalNotary.org website, social media, publications, annual conferences, seminars, online training and the NNA® Hotline, which offers immediate answers to specific questions about notarization.

In addition, the NNA offers the highest quality professional supplies, including official seals and stamps, recordkeeping journals, Notary certificates and Notary bonds.

Though dedicated primarily to educating and assisting Notaries, the NNA supports implementing effective Notary laws and informing the public about the Notary's vital role in today's society.

To learn more about the National Notary Association, visit NationalNotary.org. ∎

Index

A

Acknowledgments 27–32
Address change 6
Advertising 25–26
Affidavits 39–40
Affirmations 37–39
Apostilles 23
Application, Notary 2–3
Authentication 23–24
Authorized acts 26
Awareness 9

B

Birth certificate 33
Bond, Notary 3–4

C

Certificate, Notary 48–50
Certificate of capacity 23
Certified copies 32–34
Change of criminal record 7
Civil-law Notaries 5–6
Copies of Notary records 34
Credible identifying
  witness(es) 12–15

D

Depositions 40–41

Direct communication 8
Disqualifying interest 21

E

Electronic witnessing 59–61

F

Fees 42–43
Fines 62–66
Flags 23
Foreign languages 24–25

I

Identification documents (ID
  cards) 11–12
Identifying document signers ... 9–10
Illegal and improper acts 63–66
Immigration 25
Incomplete documents 20
In-person electronic
  notarization 53–54
Inventorying a safe-deposit
  box 34–35

J

Journal of notarial acts 45–47
Jurats 35–36
Jurisdiction 4

L

Law enforcement officers 5
Laws, Notary 67–111
Legalization 23
Liability and investigation 66
Lost or misplaced commission
 certificate 7

M

Maintenance of commission 62–63
Marriages 36–37
Minors, notarizing for 18–19
Misconduct 62–66

N

Name change 6
Notarizing for one who directs the
 Notary to sign 15–17
Notarizing for the blind 17

O

Oath of office 4
Oaths 37–39

P

Penalties 62–66
Personal appearance 8
Personal knowledge of
 identity 10–11
Prothonotary 23

Q

Qualifications 2

R

Reappointment 5
Reasonable care 47
Refusal of services 21–22
Remote online notarization 55–59
Resignation 7

S

Seal, Notary 51–52
Signature by mark 17–19

T

Term of office 5
Thumbprint 46

U

Unauthorized Notary
 practices 43–44
Unauthorized practice of law 22

V

Verifying a vehicle identification
 number 41–42

W

Willingness 9
Wills 22–23

Notes

Notes

Notes

Notes

Notes